No Bull Music Theory For Guitarists

Master the Essential Knowledge All Guitarists Need to Know

by James Shipway

No Bull Music Theory for Guitarists
by James Shipway

Published by Headstock Books
headstockbooks.com

Book Cover Design by ebooklaunch.com

Paperback ISBN: 978-1-914453-10-6
Hardcover ISBN: 978-1-914453-12-0 / 978-1-914453-13-7
Ebook ISBN: 978-1-914453-11-3

Search for 'james shipway guitar' on YouTube and
subscribe for hours of free video lessons!

Join my online community at **totalguitarlab.com** and
get instant access to *all* my premium guitar courses *plus* live training,
workshops and Q&A sessions.

Contents

Introduction 1
How Should You Use This Book? 3
Chapter 1: The Musical Alphabet 5
Chapter 2: Tones and Semitones 11
Chapter 3: Major Scale 14
Chapter 4: Major and Minor Triads 20
Chapter 5: Major Scale Intervals 29
Chapter 6: Chromatic Intervals 35
Chapter 7: Major Keys (Part 1) 42
Chapter 8: Major Keys (Part 2) 49
Chapter 9: Understanding Chord Progressions 61
Chapter 10: Pentatonic Scales 68
Chapter 11: The Natural Minor Scale 76
Chapter 12: Minor Key Basics 81
Final Words 93
Free Video and Audio Lessons 94
Useful Chord Shapes 95
Useful Resources 100

Introduction

Hello, James here and welcome to the first book in my ***Music Theory for Guitarists*** series!

This series is designed to give you all the essential music theory knowledge guitarists need to know.

Back when I was a self-taught 18 year old guitar player struggling to make sense of everything, I thought that actually understanding the music you played was for some sort of 'elite breed' of musician.

These guys and girls seemed to speak a different language, a language which I felt I'd never be able to understand.

You see, unlike them I hadn't done the courses and exams, I didn't have any music qualifications and I'd never had music lessons. I just liked playing the guitar.

And when anyone talked about intervals, triads, keys, modes, the circle of fifths, modulation, or anything else like that, I'd feel uneasy, inferior and confused.

I felt like these musicians were somehow 'special'. I felt like they were different to me.

What was I thinking?!

They weren't, they'd simply had someone explain everything to them in an easy way that made sense.

As for me, I'd been struggling with a bunch of misleading books full of big confusing words and learning all the wrong stuff in the wrong order!

No wonder I felt lost...

I wrote this series of three theory books so that no guitarist needs to feel the same way I did.

I've taught the material in these books to thousands of musicians around the world both in person and via my website and I'm here to tell you this: learning about music theory doesn't need to be scary, difficult or confusing. Anyone can learn to understand the music they play.

With these bite-sized chapters telling you what you need to know and without all the badly explained and confusing words and language, you can learn and understand in minutes, things which confuse most guitar players for years!

Once you grasp the simple concepts I show you here, you'll find everything in the music you play makes much more sense. You'll also discover new possibilities in your playing and composing and you'll be able to understand and communicate with other musicians much more easily.

I don't know about you, but I think things are so much more enjoyable when you understand them and can see exactly what's going on!

How Should You Use This Book?

For *amazing* results with this book, I'd suggest following these 5 simple tips:

1. Start at the beginning and go through the chapters in order

Even if everything is a bit basic for you at first, start at the beginning. The early chapters are only short and going through them will make sure there aren't any gaps in your understanding which could hold you up later.

I've chosen to cover the absolute basics. This is because I've found *not* understanding the absolute basics is what holds *most* players up and makes everything further along confusing. I want to *make sure* that this doesn't happen to you!

2. Test yourself with the quiz at the end of each chapter

Use the quiz questions to check you've understood everything in the chapter. The chapters build on each other, so it's important to grasp each one before you progress to the next.

You'll find the answers to the quiz questions at the end of each chapter so that you can see how you did.

3. Do the practical exercises

You'll find various practical exercises to do throughout the book. These will help you see how the theory you're studying relates to the guitar. These are written out using guitar fretboard diagrams and chord boxes. There's no need to read written music!

Note: I've given you suggested chord shapes for some exercises in the later chapters of the book. These simply give you *one* option which will work; use different shapes to the ones shown if you wish to.

4. Study each chapter more than once

I've done my best to make everything easy to understand, but some things will take more than one reading to sink in.

Remember, there is no rush ... this book isn't going anywhere!

Study each chapter several times if necessary, so that what it is teaching you becomes second nature. Then you'll have that knowledge at your fingertips and ready to use in the music you play.

5. Look for examples... and experiment!

Look for the concepts covered in this book being used in the music you listen to and play. Hear it in action!

Start analysing things like keys and chord progressions, scales and intervals. See how they are used in other people's music and how you can use them to make music of your own.

If it sounds a bit intimidating right now, don't worry, by the end of this book you will have what you need to do this!

Also experiment with using these concepts to make up songs / chord sequences / melodies / riffs etc of your own. This will take your understanding to a whole new level because you'll start to learn *how* to use it in a way that sounds good to you.

So, follow these tips as you go along and you'll soon be seeing big changes in the way you understand music!

BONUS TIP: Use the free audio lessons!

To help you get even better results with ***No Bull Music Theory for Guitarists*** I've turned these lessons into downloadable audio files. This makes each lesson *even easier* to learn from. Save them onto a device like your phone and you can brush up on your music theory in the car, travelling on a bus or train or walking the dog!

To get your free optional audio lessons go here:

jamesshipwayguitar.com/theory

That's it for now, time to get started on our journey of musical discovery.

So good luck, have fun and let's jump into the first chapter of ***No Bull Music Theory for Guitarists***!

Chapter 1: The Musical Alphabet

Amazing though it may seem, all music is made from only 12 notes! These 12 notes are often called the *chromatic scale*.

This can sound a bit intimidating and confusingly, 'chromatic' can mean other things too in music, so I like to refer to the 12 notes as the 'musical alphabet'.

The musical alphabet is the basis of everything else I'm going to show you in this book so it's important that you understand it.

Luckily, it's pretty simple to get to grips with.

Here's What You Need To Know About the Musical Alphabet...

There are 7 letter names used in music:

A, B, C, D, E, F and G

These letters are used to describe 7 of the 12 notes in the musical alphabet.

These 7 notes just with letter names are often called the 'natural' notes.

So, if that accounts for 7 of the notes we use when we play music, what about the remaining 5 notes?

These are the flats and sharps.

The symbol for sharp is '#' (e.g. *C sharp* is written C#).

The symbol for a flat is '*b*' (e.g. *B flat* is written B*b*).

Sharps and flats sit *in between* the natural notes in the musical alphabet.

Any sharp can also be described as a flat. In other words, although the note is the same, it has two different names which we can use to describe it.

For example, the note that sits between C and D can either be given a sharp name *or* a flat name - we can call it C# *or* D*b*.

Which one you'd use depends on a few things we don't need to go into right now (it doesn't normally matter anyway).

So, if we write out the complete musical alphabet including the sharps and flats it looks like this:

A - A#/B*b* - B - C - C#/D*b* - D - D#/E*b* - E - F - F#/G*b* - G - G#/A*b*

Notice we're using both the sharp and the flat names for the notes that sit in between the natural notes.

The best way to visualise the musical alphabet is on a keyboard (don't worry, you don't need to be able to play piano or keyboards!).

The natural notes are the white keys. The sharps and flats are the black keys in between.

Let's take a look:

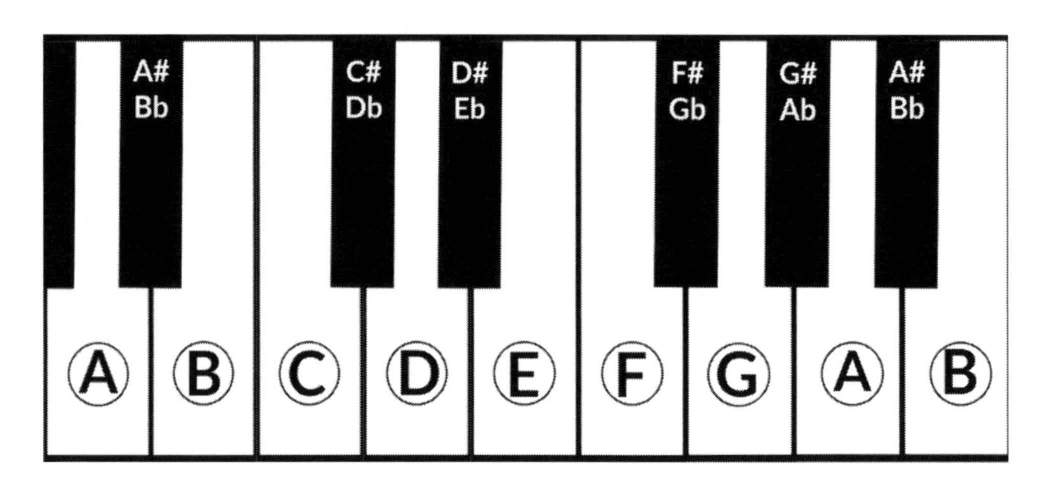

Now you might have noticed something strange here;

There is no # or *b* note in between B and C or between E and F.

This is just the way our musical language has evolved.

So, remember there is no B# or C*b* or E# or F*b*.

And that's the musical alphabet!

<u>Try These Practical Exercises:</u>

Grab your guitar and take a look at the musical alphabet in action!

Exercise 1

1. Start on the note A at the 5th fret on the low E string
2. Move up 1 fret to the 6th fret. You're now on the next note in the musical alphabet (A# or B*b*)
3. Go up 1 fret to the 7th fret. You're now on the next note: B
4. Keep going saying each note name as you go until you reach A again up at the 17th fret.
5. You just played all 12 notes in the musical alphabet along the E string

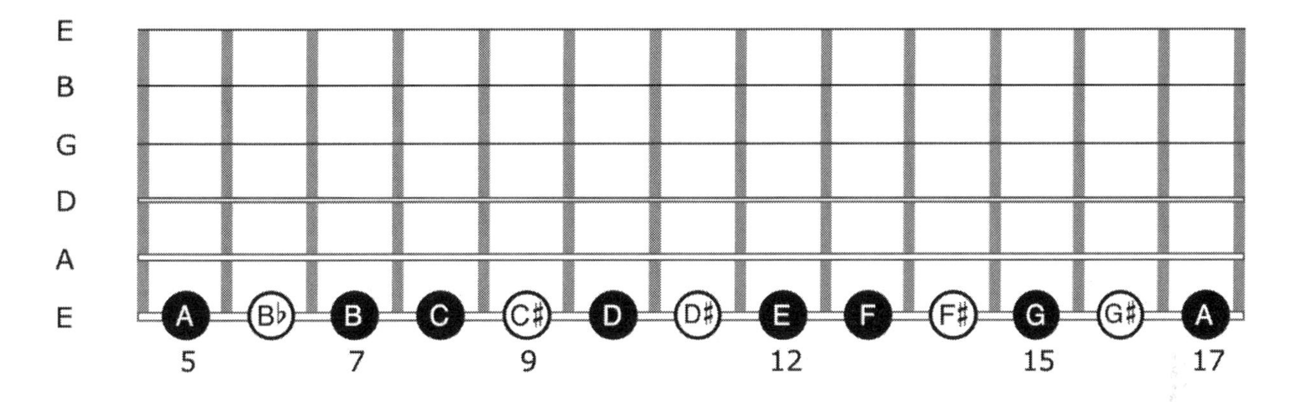

Exercise 2

You can start the alphabet from any note. The order of the notes is always the same. Let's see this in action now:

1. Start on the note C at the 3rd fret on the A string
2. Move up 1 fret to the 4th fret. You're now on the next note in the musical alphabet (C# or D*b*)
3. Go up 1 fret to the 5th fret. You're now on the next note: D
4. Keep going saying each note name as you go until you reach C again up at the 15th fret
5. You just played all 12 notes in the musical alphabet along the A string

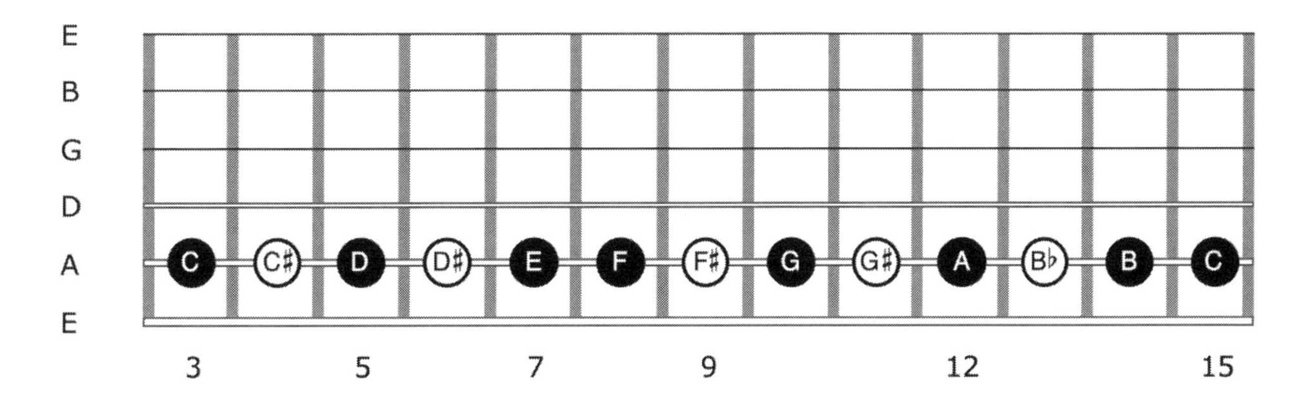

Of course, the musical alphabet doesn't only apply to the E and A strings! These 12 notes are also found on the other strings on the guitar.

Study the following fretboard diagram and you'll see the same 12 notes, in the same order on all 6 strings:

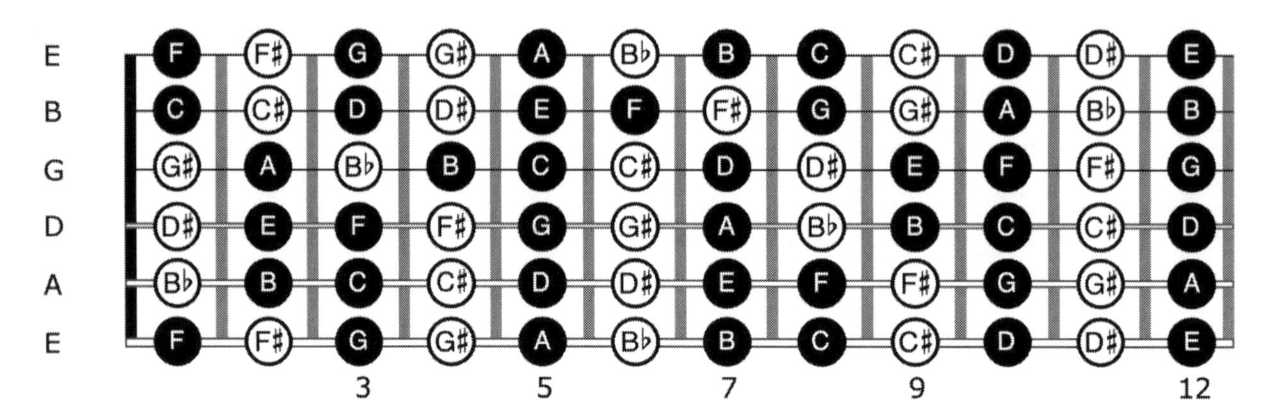

Should you learn where all the notes are on the guitar?

If you want to, but it's not absolutely essential right now. Just be sure you understand *why* the notes on the guitar are found where they are.

That's most of what you need to know about the musical alphabet...

Before you move on, make sure you have a thorough understanding of what we've covered in this chapter. The musical alphabet is the foundation of everything else you're going to learn about in this book so, it's very important that you understand it.

Test yourself using the questions that follow and when you're ready move on to the next chapter where you'll be learning about ***tones*** and ***semi-tones***!

Now, Test Yourself on the Musical Alphabet!

The musical alphabet contains __________ notes.

The musical alphabet is also called the _________________ scale.

The notes A, B, C, D, E, F and G are the ______________ notes.

The symbol we use for a sharp is ____________.

The symbol we use for a flat is ____________.

There is no flat or sharp note in between ______ and ______.

There is also no flat or sharp note in between the notes _____and_____.

The note in between G and A is _____ sharp or ______ flat.

Between D and E you get the note _________ or ________.

Here's the musical alphabet starting on C. Fill in the following missing notes. Use either the sharp or the flat note where appropriate:

C - _ - _ - _ - _ - _ - _ - G - _ - _ - _ - _ - C

Find out how you did by checking the answers on the next page!

Find Out How You Did!

*The musical alphabet contains **12** notes.*

*The musical alphabet is also called the **chromatic** scale.*

*The notes A, B, C, D, E, F and G are the **natural** notes.*

*The symbol we use for a sharp is **#.***

*The symbol we use for a flat is **b.***

*There is no flat or sharp note in between **B and C.***

*There is also no flat or sharp note in between the notes **E and F.***

*The note in between G and A is **G sharp** or **A flat.***

*Between D and E you get the note **D#** or **Eb.***

Starting on C the musical alphabet looks like this:

C - C#/Db - D - D#/E*b* - E - F - F#/G*b* - G - G#/A*b* - A - A#/B*b* - B – C

Chapter 2: Tones and Semitones

Tones...semitones....half steps...whole steps....

You've probably heard of them, but do you know what they are?

In this short chapter we'll take a quick look at what tones and semitones are. You need to know about them, you'll be using them a lot when we examine scales and chords.

But don't worry, tones and semitones are *really* easy to understand.

Let's get started!

Here's What You Need To Know About Tones & Semitones...

Tones and semitones are simply musical 'distances' or 'steps' between two notes.

A *semitone* is a distance of 1 fret.

If you moved a note, scale or chord shape up 1 fret from say the 2nd fret to the 3rd fret, you could say you were moving it *up a semitone*.

A *tone* is a distance of 2 frets.

Let's say you move a note, a scale or a chord shape down 2 frets from the 7th fret to the 5th fret, you could say you were moving it *down a tone*.

Sometimes tones are referred to as *whole steps* and semitones are referred to as *half steps*.

Can you spot the semitone and the tone on the low E string in the following diagram?

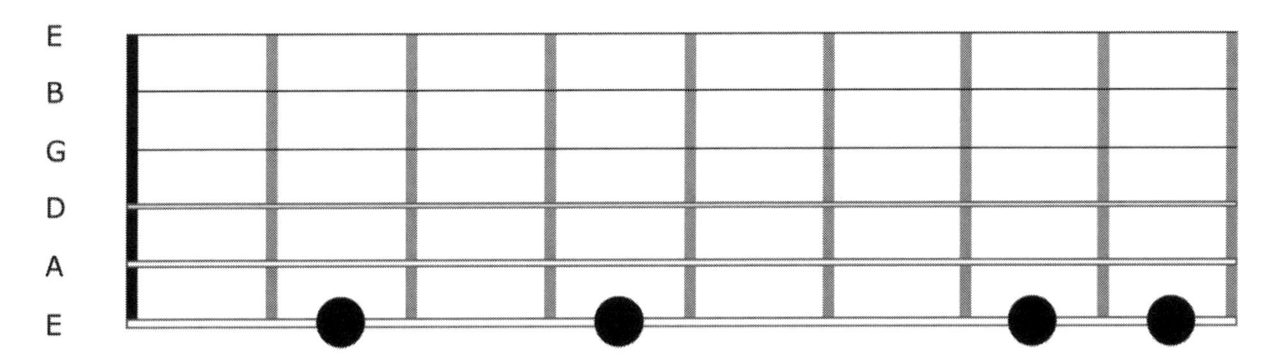

That's most of what you need to know about tones and semitones...

I told you tones and semitones were easy to understand!

All you need to remember is that a semitone is 1 fret and a tone is 2 frets and you've got it covered.

Test yourself using the questions that follow and when you're ready I'll see you in the next chapter where we'll be looking at the major scale.

Now, Test Yourself on Tones & Semitones!

A semitone is a distance of __________ fret.

A tone is a distance of __________ frets.

A semitone can also be called a _______________.

A tone can also be called a _________________.

Find out how you did by checking the answers on the next page!

Find Out How You Did!

*A semitone is a distance of **1** fret.*

*A tone is a distance of **2** frets.*

*A semitone can also be called a **half step**.*

*A tone can also be called a **whole step**.*

Chapter 3: Major Scale

One of the most important musical tools you need to know about is the **major scale**.

Depending on the music we perform, we may not use the major scale that much when we play. We might use scales like minor pentatonic and major pentatonic scales instead (we'll be studying these later).

So, you might be wondering *why* we need to study the major scale at all.

It's because knowing about the major scale will help you to understand loads of other crucial things like chords, keys, intervals, chord progressions and other scales. We can also use the major scale to build things like seventh chords and modes, we'll be looking at doing this in ***Music Theory for Guitarists, Volume 2***.

So even if you don't end up using the major scale that much in your playing, learning about it is an essential step towards understanding other things which you will use and play a lot.

So, stick with me as we 'deep dive' into the major scale and I show you everything you need to know about it.

Let's go!

Here's What You Need To Know About the Major Scale...

Before we go any further let's define what we mean when we talk about a 'scale'.

You could find dozens of different definitions of what a scale is (some of them way too confusing!) but I like this one:

A scale is a collection or set of notes with a particular sound which we use as a tool to create music

There are lots of different scales in music, giving us lots of different sounds. This is why some music sounds uplifting and happy and other music sounds dark or scary.

But of all the possible scales we could look at, probably the most important one you need to understand is the **7 note** scale known as the ***major scale***.

So, what is the Major Scale?

If you asked 10 guitar players this question, you'd probably get 10 different answers!

Let's look at the simple (and correct!) answer to this question. Grab your guitar and do the following:

Play the **3rd fret** on the **high E string**. You're playing a G note.

Now move it up a **tone** (that's 2 frets, remember?) to the **5th fret**

Now move it up another **tone** to the **7th fret**

Now move it up a **semitone** (that's 1 fret, remember?)

Now move it up a **tone**

Move it up another **tone**

Move it up one more **tone**

Go up a **semitone**

That's it!

You should be up at the **15th** fret on the note G one **octave** higher than where you started (more on octaves in a minute!).

You just played a G major scale along one string, like in the following diagram:

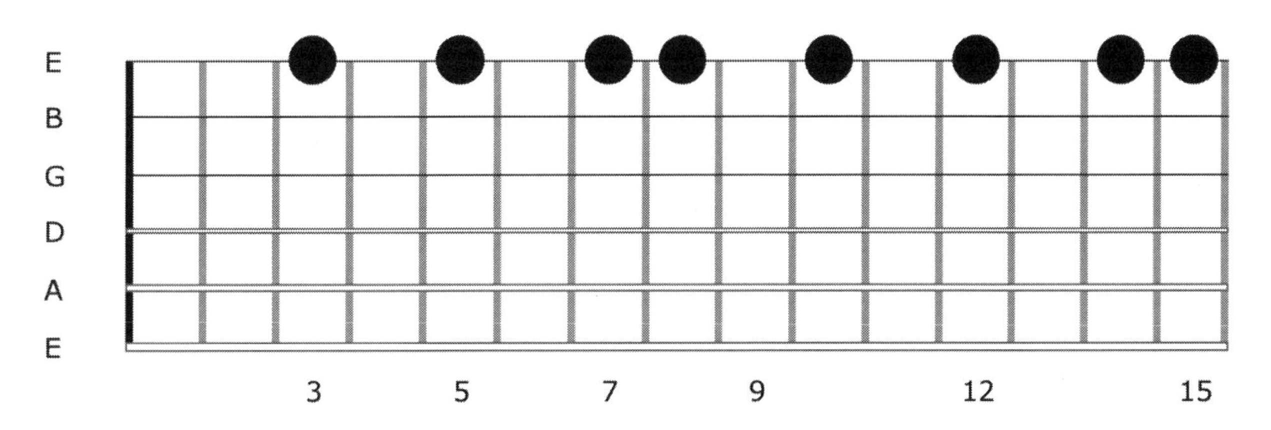

You see, the major scale is really just a sequence of **tones** and **semitones** arranged in a **certain order**:

TONE - TONE - SEMITONE - TONE - TONE - TONE - SEMITONE

Follow this formula or 'recipe' of tones and semitones and you get a major scale.

Some points to note:

The note you start the formula on determines which major scale you get.

You just started on a G note, so the major scale you got was the G major scale.
If you had started on a D and followed the formula, you'd have got a D major scale instead.

This starting note is called the **root note**, sometimes you might hear it called the **tonic**.

If you started on any note on the guitar and played this sequence of tones and semitones, you'd be playing a major scale.

It's a good idea to memorise this tone and semitone sequence, it'll help you out in all sorts of situations!

Now, you might be wondering...

Can you change the tone/semitone sequence?

No! The pattern *must* stay the same. If it's changed the resulting scale is not a major scale. You've changed the 'recipe'...so you'll get a different scale.

How many major scales are there?

We know from the musical alphabet chapter that there are just **12 notes**. The tone/semitone formula can be played starting on *any* of these giving **12 possible major scales.**

I've seen major scale patterns on guitar played across the strings. Why are we only playing them along 1 string here?

Playing along one string makes it *really* easy to see the structure of the scale and the tone/semitone formula in action. This makes it much easier to understand what the major scale actually is. Major scales can be arranged into scale fingerings which go *across* the strings of the guitar instead of *along* the strings. However, whether you play a major scale along a string or across several strings it will still contain the same 7 notes!

So, what do I actually do with the major scale?

Lots of things! We'll be discussing them later in this book. For now, it's just about understanding what the major scale is.

You mentioned an 'octave'. What is this?

After you've played through the tone/semitone formula you end up on the same note you began on but higher up the neck. This note has the same name as the starting note but is 'one whole major scale away' from where you started. We could describe this note as being 'one octave higher' than the starting note.

One final thing on the major scale...

Different major scales contain different notes. In fact, although some major scales are very similar, no two major scales contain the exact same 7 notes.

If you saw a list of the notes in each major scale, you'd see that all of them apart from the C major scale contain at least one flat (*b*) or sharp (#) note.

The G major scale for example contains an F#.

The B*b* major scale contains 2 flats (B*b* and E*b*).

Sometimes this confuses people, but the explanation is really quite simple.

When we follow the tone/semitone pattern starting from any note except C, we just happen to land on at least one sharp or flat note. This is just the way it works out and is why most major scales contain at least one flat or a sharp note.

Try These Practical Exercises:

Grab a guitar and use these exercises to play major scales along one string. This is the perfect way to see the tone/semitone formula in action.

Exercise 1

1. Start on the note A at the 5th fret on the low E string
2. Follow the formula of tones/semitones
3. You just played an A major scale along the E string

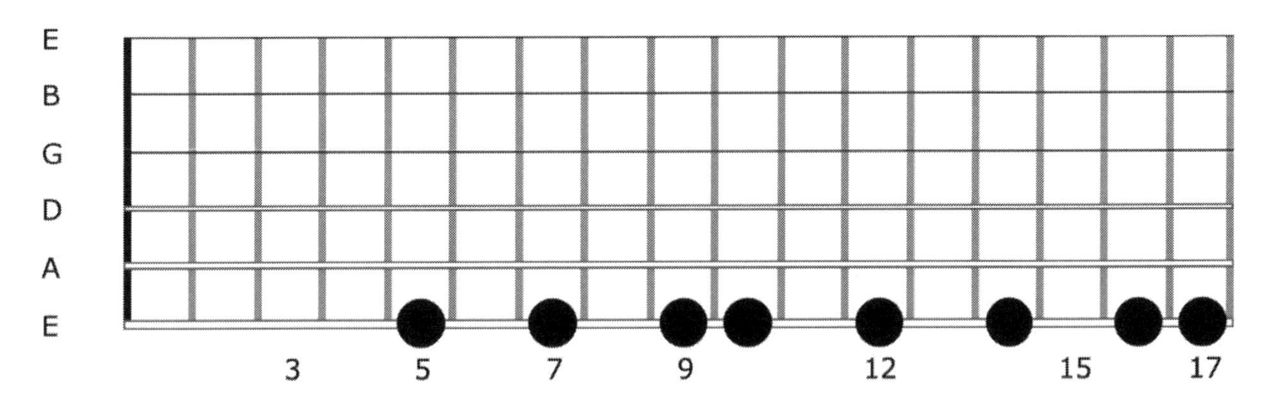

Exercise 2

1. Start on the note C at the 3rd fret on the A string
2. Follow the formula of tones/semitones
3. You just played a C major scale along the A string

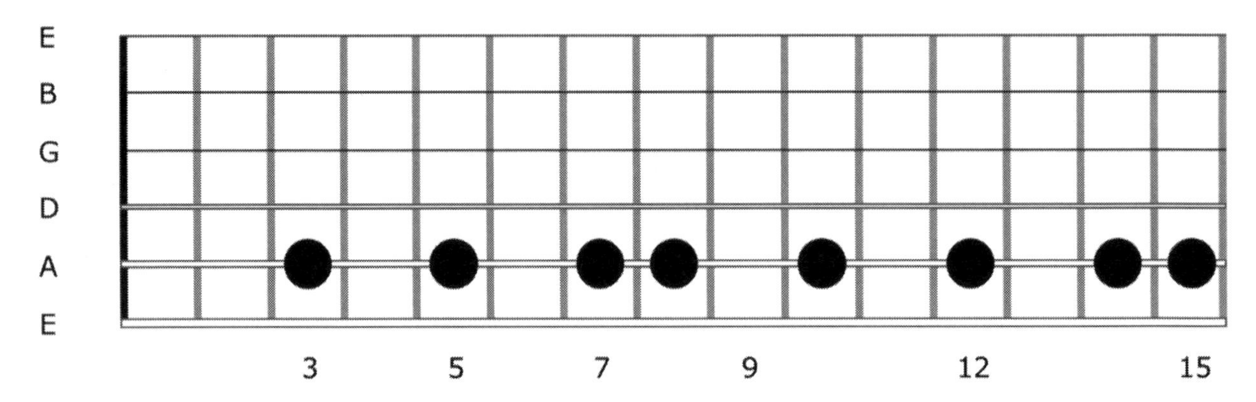

And that's *most* of what you need to know about the major scale (for now anyway!)

We'll be returning to the major scale many times in this book, so for now focus on getting an understanding of the basics as outlined in this chapter.

Test yourself with the questions coming up next and apply the practical exercises to help you get a solid grasp of the theory here.

You'll find out in the next chapter how to use the major scale to build major and minor triads!

Now, Test Yourself on the Major Scale!

The major scale contains __________ notes.

The formula of tones and semitones used to get a major scale is:
______________________________.

The note we start the formula on is often called the _____________ note or _______________.

Can the pattern of tones/semitones be changed? _______________

How many possible major scales are there? _______________

All major scales apart from the C major scale contain at least one ________ or _________ note.

When you've played through the scale you end up on the starting note one ________________ higher.

Find out how you did by checking the answers on the next page!

Find Out How You Did!

*The major scale contains **7** notes.*

The formula of tones and semitones used to get a major scale is:

TONE - TONE - SEMITONE - TONE - TONE - TONE - SEMITONE

*The note we start the formula on is often called the **root** note or **tonic.***

Can the pattern of tones/semitones be changed?

No! It must stay the same or the scale is not a major scale anymore.

How many possible major scales are there?

*There are **12** major scales.*

*All major scales apart from the C major scale contain at least one **sharp** or **flat** note.*

*When you've played through the scale you end up on the starting note one **octave** higher.*

Chapter 4: Major and Minor Triads

A 'chord shape' is quite likely the very first thing you learned when you started playing guitar!

But even though we use chords and 'chord shapes' a lot, many players don't really understand what a chord *actually is*.

Knowing about basic chords and understanding the differences between them helps you become better at soloing, rhythm guitar, creating your own songs and riffs and just helps you to understand how music works a whole lot better!

The simplest chords to understand are called **triads**. These are what we are going to be studying in this chapter.

So, let's get started!

Here's What You Need To Know About Triads...

A triad is a type of **chord**.

Think of a chord as:

A group of notes played together to give us a certain sound

How many notes make up a chord?

It varies. Some chords, like the power chords or '5' chords we often use on guitar, only contain two notes. Other more complex chords may contain 5 or 6 notes.

Many common chords contain just **3 notes**. These are called **triads** and the two most common types of triad are **major** and **minor**.

What is a *Major* Triad?

Making a major triad is easy!

You simply group together the first note (or root), 3rd note and 5th note from any major scale.

So, the formula looks like this:

Root + 3rd + 5th = major triad

Let's look at how this works in practice.

Here are the notes in the **G major scale**:

G A B C D E F#

Can you work out the notes in a G major triad?

If you grouped together **G** (root), **B** (3rd) and **D** (5th), then you're absolutely right!

This process of stacking the 1st, 3rd and 5th notes from a major scale to get a major triad works for all major scales:

Apply it to the F major scale you'll get an F major triad...

Apply it to the D*b* major scale you'll get a D*b* major triad...

And so on...

Let's See This In Practice...

Look at this basic G major chord shape. The notes in the chord are labelled. Even though six strings are played, this chord is still a basic G major triad. This is because it only contains three notes: G, B and D (including the open strings). We're just playing some of the notes in the triad more than once:

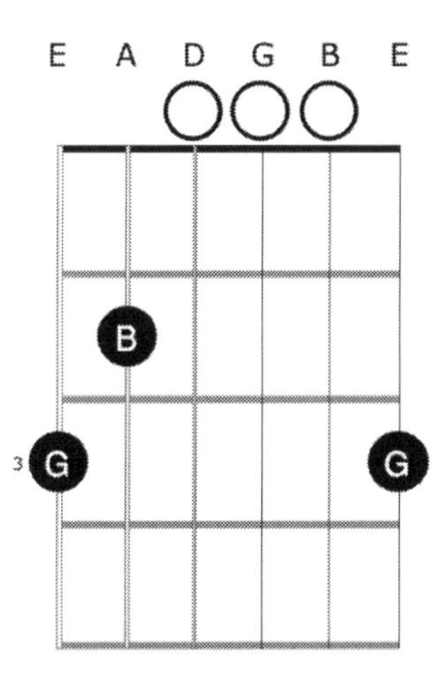

The following G major barre chord shape is also a major triad.

It too contains just the notes G, B and D, but as in the other chord shape, some of the notes are played more than once:

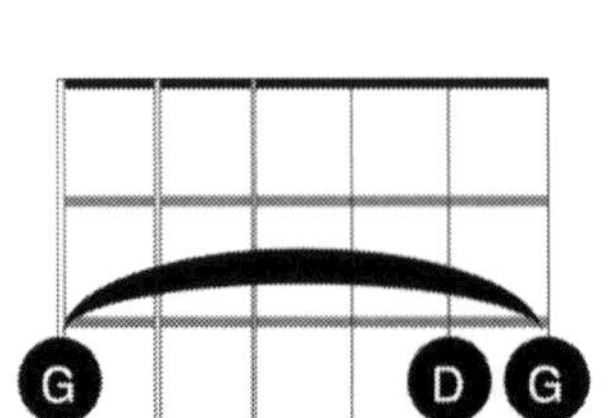

When we talk about major triads, we often leave out the 'major' part of the name. It's normally shortened just to a letter name like C, F or G.

Most of the 'beginner chord shapes' we learn when we start playing guitar, chords like E, C, A and D, are simply major triads! They may cover 4 or more strings...but they only contain 3 notes (some of the notes are just played more than once).

So, you've likely been playing 'major triads' for some time, perhaps without knowing it!

What is a *Minor* Triad?

A minor triad is almost the same as a major triad.

There is just one **important difference**.

The first note (or root), 3rd note and 5th note are grouped together like before...

But the 3rd is then flattened by 1 fret or a semitone

So, the formula looks like this:

Root + *b3rd* + 5th = minor triad

Here are the notes in the **G major scale** again:

G A B C D E F#

If we flatten the 3rd (B) it becomes B*b* (the note a semitone / or 1 fret below B in the musical alphabet).

So, the notes in a G minor triad are **G** (root), **B*b*** (flat 3rd) and **D** (5th).

Compare this G minor barre chord to the G major shape shown a moment ago. You can see the B has been flattened by 1 fret to get B*b*.

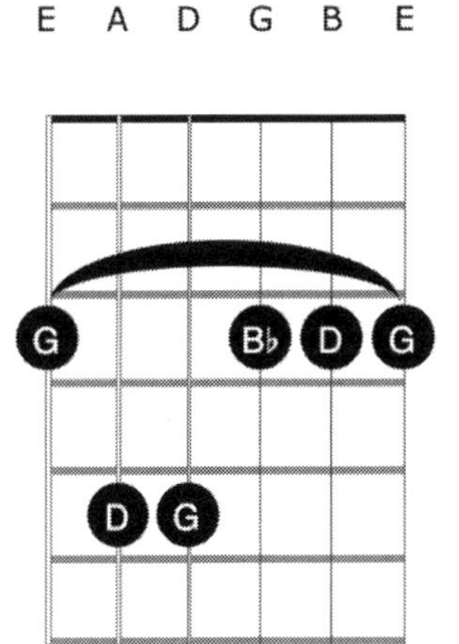

The **'flattened 3rd' is <u>the</u> note** which makes the triad minor.

In fact, any minor scale, minor chord, or anything else 'minor' will have a *b*3rd in it.

It's the note that defines something as being 'minor'.

Remember this, it's very important!

<u>In Summary...</u>

The two most common types of triad are **major** and **minor**.

We get a major triad by grouping together the **1st, 3rd and 5th** notes from a major scale.

We get a minor triad by grouping together the **1st, *b*3rd and 5th** notes from a major scale.

<u>Let's Apply This Now:</u>

To clearly see the difference between major and minor triads grab your guitar and do these simple exercises. If you haven't got a guitar on you right now then imagine yourself doing them in your mind's eye.

Exercise 1

1. Play an E chord down at the open position

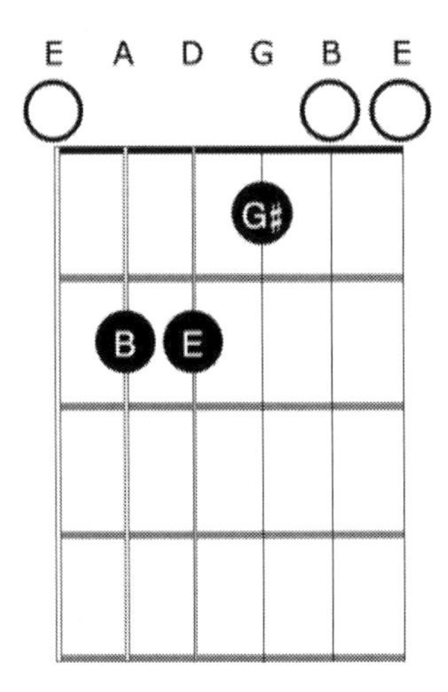

2. The 3rd (G#) is on the G string at the 1st fret (probably played with your 1st finger)
3. Change it to E minor

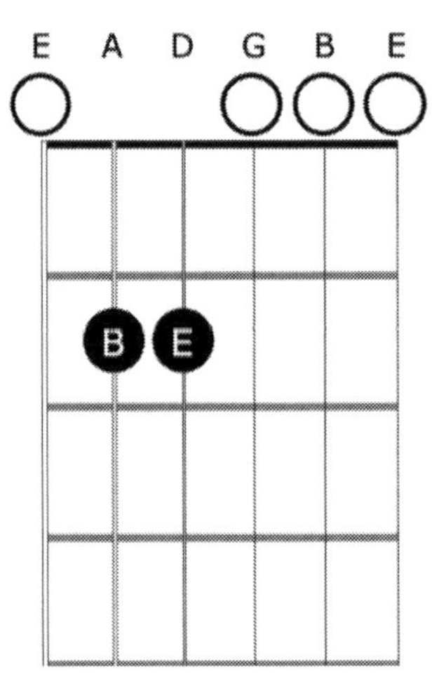

Can you see the 3rd 'flattening' to become the open G string?

Exercise 2

1. Play a D chord at the open position. The 3rd (F#) is on the top E string, 2nd fret

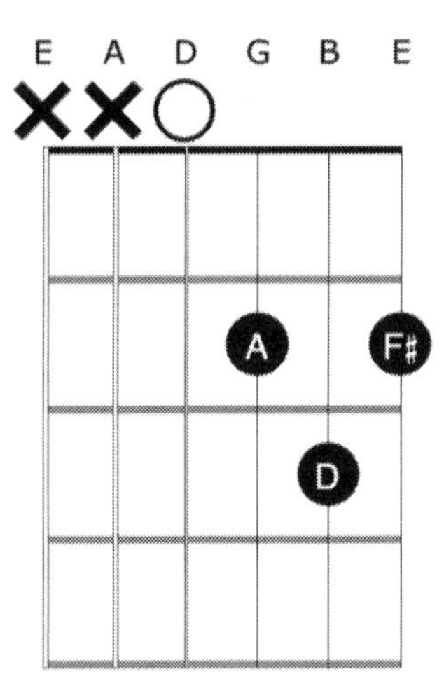

2. Change it to a D minor chord shape

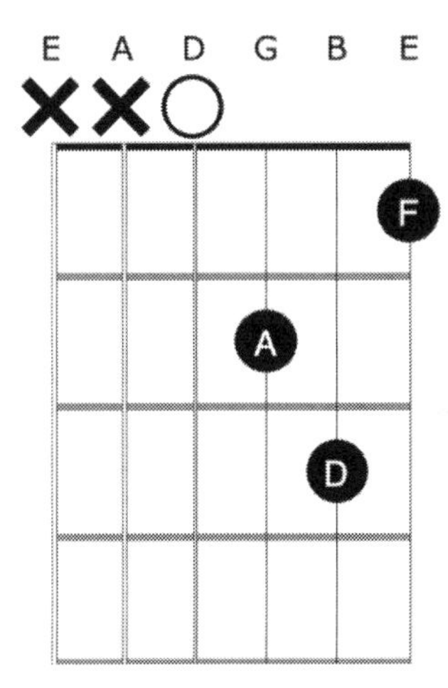

3. See how the 3rd drops down to the 1st fret to become flattened to F?

Now, you might be wondering...

That's chords...but what about major and minor scales?

We'll be looking at this in more detail later. A simple answer is that any 'major type' scale will have an 'unflattened' 3rd in it. Any 'minor' type scale will have a *b*3rd.

For example, G **major** pentatonic contains a **B** (3rd note from G major scale).

G **minor** pentatonic has a **B*b*** (flattened 3rd from G major scale).

Don't worry about pentatonics for the moment, we'll come to those later.

Can a triad start on any note?

Yes. In the musical alphabet there are 12 notes, making 12 possible major and 12 possible minor triads.

Are there other triads I need to know about?

There are two other types of triad: diminished and augmented, but they are pretty rarely used so I've left them out for now.

Are barre chords triads?

Any chord that is simply major or minor is a triad. It doesn't matter which shape you use to play it on the guitar.

Chords with longer names like **maj7** (*major seven*), **m7** (*minor seven*), **add9** (*add nine*) and **m11** (minor11) are *not* triads because they contain more than 3 notes. Don't worry about these for now, we'll be looking at all these kinds of chords in volumes 2 & 3 of this book series.

What about power chords like E5, A5, C5 and D5 etc?

This confused me for years! But the answer is actually very simple.

Power chords like E5, A5, C5 or D5 don't have a 3rd at all!

They only contain the root and the 5th from the scale. The note that distinguishes between major and minor is missing so a power chord can be treated as major *or* minor. In other words, a G5 power chord can stand in for a G major or a G minor chord in a song!

That's most of what you need to know about major and minor triads...

Of course, there is much more you can learn about the topic of chords than just what I've told you in this chapter.

But make no mistake, understanding triads is an essential first step.

Why?

Because 99% of other chords are simply a triad with some extra notes added! So, knowing about and understanding triads will make it much easier to understand more complex chords further down the road.

Test yourself using the questions that follow and when you're ready I'll see you in the next chapter where you'll be learning all about intervals.

See you then...

Now, Test Yourself on Triads!

Triads are chords containing __________ notes.

What is the formula for a **major** triad?

____

What is the formula for a **minor** triad?

____

What is the only difference between a major and minor triad?

____

The notes in the D major scale are:

D E F# G A B C#

What are the notes in a D major triad? _____________

What are the notes in a D minor triad? _____________

The notes in the B*b* major scale are:

B*b* C D E*b* F G A

What are the notes in a B*b* major triad? _____________

What are the notes in a B*b* minor triad? _____________

Are power chords or '5' chords triads? _____________

Are power chords major or minor? _____________

Find out how you did by checking the answers on the next page!

Find Out How You Did!

Triads *are chords containing* ***3*** *notes.*

The formula for a ***major*** *triad is* ***Root + 3rd + 5th*** *from a major scale.*

The formula for a ***minor*** *triad is* ***Root + b3rd + 5th*** *from a major scale.*

The only difference between a major and minor triad is the ***flattened 3rd*** *in the minor triad.*

The notes in the D major scale are:

D E F# G A B C#

The notes in a D major triad are ***D F# and A****.*

The notes in a D minor triad are ***D F and A****.*

The notes in the Bb major scale are:

B*b* C D E*b* F G A

The notes in a Bb major triad are ***Bb D and F****.*

The notes in a Bb minor triad are ***Bb Db and F****.*

Power chords or '5' chords are ***not triads*** *because they only contain 2 notes.*

Power chords are ***neither major nor minor****! They don't contain the 3rd or the b3rd so can be treated as either.*

Chapter 5: Major Scale Intervals

Musicians talk often talk about 'intervals' and if you don't know what they are it can make things pretty confusing!

So, in this lesson we're going to take a detailed look at what we mean when we talk about intervals in music.

The first bit of good news is that intervals are actually very simple to understand.

The second bit of good news is that when you know about intervals - chords, scales, keys and loads of other things you use all the time when making music will make a lot more sense!

So, investing a bit of time into learning about intervals is well worth the effort.

Let's get started!

Here's What You Need to Know About Intervals...

An interval is simply:

The distance between two notes

These distances are described as a number, for example *'a third'* or *'a seventh'*.

Sometimes another word is put before the number, as in *'major third'* or *'perfect fourth'*.

Let's take a look at what all this interval stuff is about. To do this we'll use our old friend the C major scale.

First, we'll take the C major scale and number the notes from Root (or 1) to 7 in the order that they ascend the scale:

C	D	E	F	G	A	B
Root	2	3	4	5	6	7

This means we can now describe the relationship between C and any other note by using its number, or position in the scale.

For example:

D is the *2nd* of C

This is because D is the 'second' note in the major scale.

You could also say that C to D is an ***'interval of a 2nd'***

G is the *5th* of C

This is because G is the 'fifth' note in the major scale.

You could also say that C to G is an ***'interval of a 5th'***

See how it works?

We can use this method to describe and understand how all the notes in the scale relate to C.

C to D is an interval of a ***2nd*** (or *'D is the second of C'*)

C to E is an interval of a ***3rd*** (or *'E is the third of C'*)

C to F is an interval of a ***4th*** (or *'F is the fourth of C'*)

C to G is an interval of a ***5th*** (or *'G is the fifth of C'*)

C to A is an interval of a ***6th*** (or *'A is the sixth of C'*)

C to B is an interval of a ***7th*** (or *'B is the seventh of C'*)

C to C is an interval of an ***octave*** (same note higher up!)

Here is the C major scale you played along the A string in an earlier chapter. We can now label each note with its interval number:

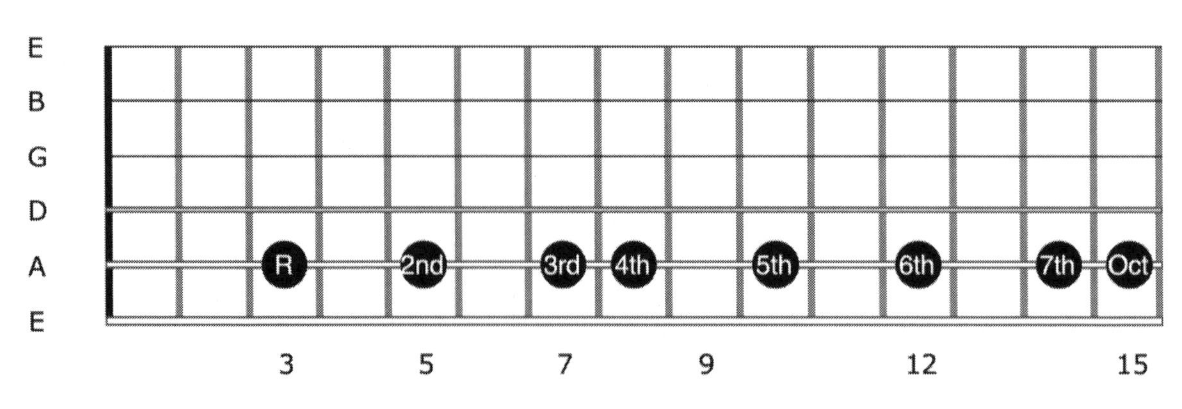

The 'Traditional' Interval Names

Sometimes words like *perfect* and *major* are added to the number to describe an interval.

For example, a musician might talk about a 'perfect 5th'.

This is the more 'traditional' way of naming intervals used in classical music education. It's good to know these too (they're not hard to understand).

Basically, all the intervals we've seen so far are *major* except for the 4th and 5th which are said to be *perfect*.

So, we could describe them like this:

C to D is an interval of a ***major 2nd*** (or *'D is the major second of C'*)

C to E is an interval of **a *major 3rd*** (or *'E is the major third of C'*)

C to F is an interval of a ***perfect 4th*** (or *'F is the perfect fourth of C'*)

C to G is an interval of a ***perfect 5th*** (or *'G is the perfect fifth of C'*)

C to A is an interval of a ***major 6th*** (or *'A is the major sixth of C'*)

C to B is an interval of a ***major 7th*** (or *'B is the major seventh of C'*)

Now, you might be wondering this...

Has all this interval stuff got anything to do with the numbers we see used in chord names?

Chords like C5, Csus4 and Cmajor7...

Or chord sequences like 'one, four, five' (written I IV V*)*

The answer is yes!

All this relates back to the basic interval theory we're looking at now. So, understanding intervals will help you understand other important things later on (some of which we'll be learning about in the coming chapters).

So that's major intervals. What about 'minor' intervals like minor 3rds?

These are what we call chromatic or 'non major scale' intervals and we'll be looking at these in the very next chapter.

What about scale patterns that go across the strings rather than along the strings?

Interval names can be used to describe the notes in a major scale no matter how you play it! In the next image you can see a common way to play a C major scale up at the 8th fret. Just as before the notes have been labelled with their interval name:

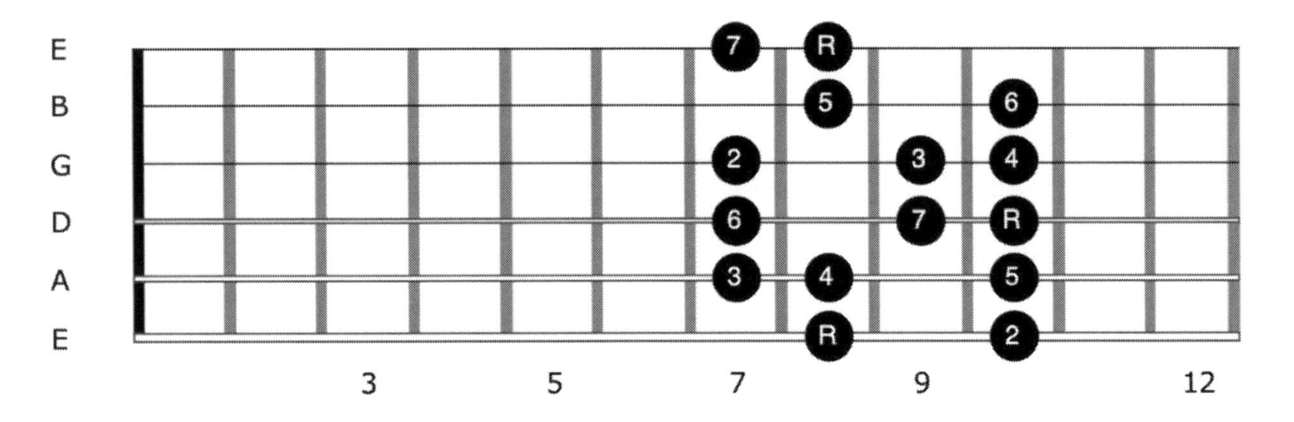

Try playing up and down this scale pattern taking note of which interval you are playing as you go. This will help this interval stuff to really sink in!

And that's most of what you need to know about major scale intervals...

There is more to intervals than just what we've discussed here, but if you understand the basic major scale intervals then the rest is pretty easy to get to grips with.

So, start by getting a thorough understanding of what we've covered in this chapter on intervals. Make sure you know the intervals as both numbers and the more traditional 'classical' names (you'll encounter them both!).

Test yourself using the questions that follow and when you're ready I'll see you in the next chapter where we'll continue our study of this topic by looking at *chromatic* intervals. This is where we'll come across all those weird interval names like diminished and augmented!

See you then...

<u>**Now, Test Yourself!**</u>

An **interval** is a way of describing the __________ between two notes.

The notes in the D major scale are:

D E F# G A B C#

What is the 4th of D? ________________

What is the 7th of D? ________________

What is the 3rd of D? ________________

What is the 6th of D? ________________

What is the 2nd of D? ________________

What is the 5th of D? ________________

The notes in the A major scale are:

A B C# D E F# G#

Provide the *'traditional'* names for the following intervals:

A to D is the interval of a ________________________.

A to G# is the interval of a ________________________.

A to B is the interval of a ________________________.

A to E is the interval of a ________________________.

A to C# is the interval of a ________________________.

A to F# is the interval of a ________________________.

A to A is the interval of an ________________________.

Find out how you did by checking the answers on the next page!

Find Out How You Did!

*An **interval** is a way of describing the **distance** between two notes.*

*The 4th of D is **G**.*

*The 7th of D is **C#**.*

*The 3rd of D is **F#**.*

*The 6th of D is **B**.*

*The 2nd of D is **E**.*

*The 5th of D is **A**.*

*A to D is the interval of a **perfect 4th**.*

*A to G# is the interval of a **major 7th**.*

*A to B is the interval of a **major 2nd**.*

*A to E is the interval of a **perfect 5th**.*

*A to C# is the interval of a **major 3rd**.*

*A to F# is the interval of a **major 6th**.*

*A to A is the interval of an **octave**.*

Chapter 6: Chromatic Intervals

In the previous lesson we looked at the major scale intervals.

Now it's time to expand on this by looking at what are often called *chromatic* intervals.

These might sound a bit scary, but if you understand your major scale intervals then they're simple to get to grips with.

When you understand what's in this lesson, you'll know most of what you'll ever need to know about intervals.

Here's What You Need To Know About Chromatic Intervals...

We can think of a ***chromatic interval*** as:

A major scale interval which has been sharpened or flattened by a semitone

It really is as simple as that.

Let's revisit the C major scale and have a quick reminder of the major scale intervals from the last lesson:

C	D	E	F	G	A	B
Root	2	3	4	5	6	7

C to D is an interval of a ***major 2nd*** (or *'D is the second of C'*).

C to E is an interval of a ***major 3rd*** (or *'E is the third of C'*).

C to F is an interval of a ***perfect 4th*** (or *'F is the fourth of C'*).

C to G is an interval of a ***perfect 5th*** (or *'G is the fifth of C'*).

C to A is an interval of a ***major 6th*** (or *'A is the sixth of C'*).

C to B is an interval of a ***major 7th*** (or *'B is the seventh of C'*).

We saw this laid out along the A string on the guitar as follows:

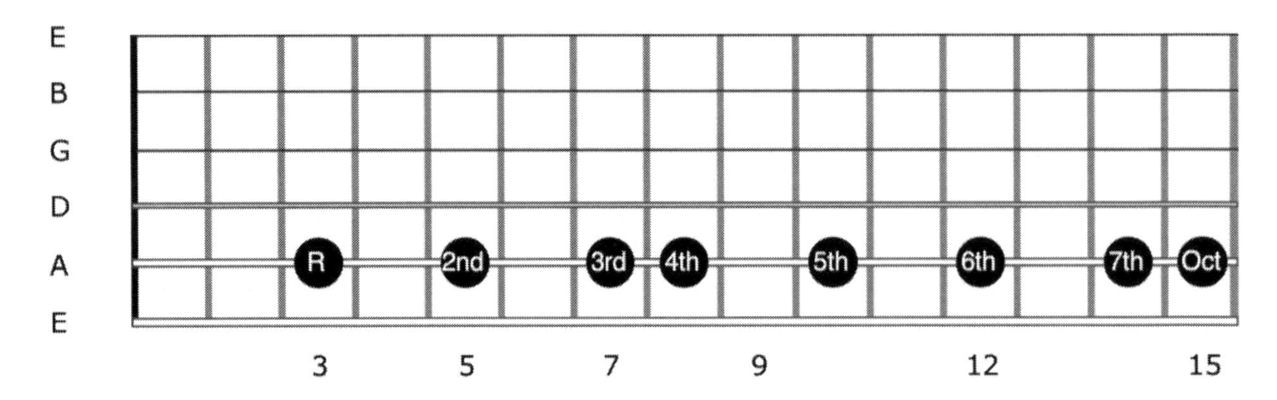

It's time to build on your interval knowledge now.

Let's say you wanted to describe the relationship between **C** and **D*b*** using an interval name.

We know that **D** is the 2nd of **C**, so we could describe **D*b*** as being the *'flattened 2nd of **C**'*.

In other words, we describe chromatic intervals as flattened or sharpened 'variations' of the major scale intervals from the last lesson.

Sometimes you'll see these written as the interval number with a flat or sharp sign before it like this:

***b*2nd** or **b2** = *flattened second*

***b*7th** or **b7** = *flattened 7th*

#5th or **#5** = *sharpened 5th*

Make sense?

Let's use this method to label all the possible chromatic intervals:

C to D*b* is an interval of a ***flattened 2nd*** (or *'Db is the b2nd of C'*).

C to D# is an interval of a ***sharpened 2nd*** (or *'D# is #2nd of C'*).

C to E*b* is an interval of a ***flattened 3rd*** (or *'Eb is the b3rd of C'*).

C to F# is an interval of a ***sharpened 4th*** (or *'F# is the #4th of C'*).

C to G*b* is an interval of a ***flattened 5th*** (or *'Gb is the b5th of C'*).

C to G# is an interval of a ***sharpened 5th*** (or *'G# is the #5th of C'*).

C to A*b* is an interval of a ***flattened 6th*** (or *'Ab is the b6th of C'*).

C to B*b* is an interval of a ***flattened 7th*** (or *'Bb is the b7th of C'*).

Here is the fretboard diagram from earlier in this chapter. The chromatic intervals have now been added:

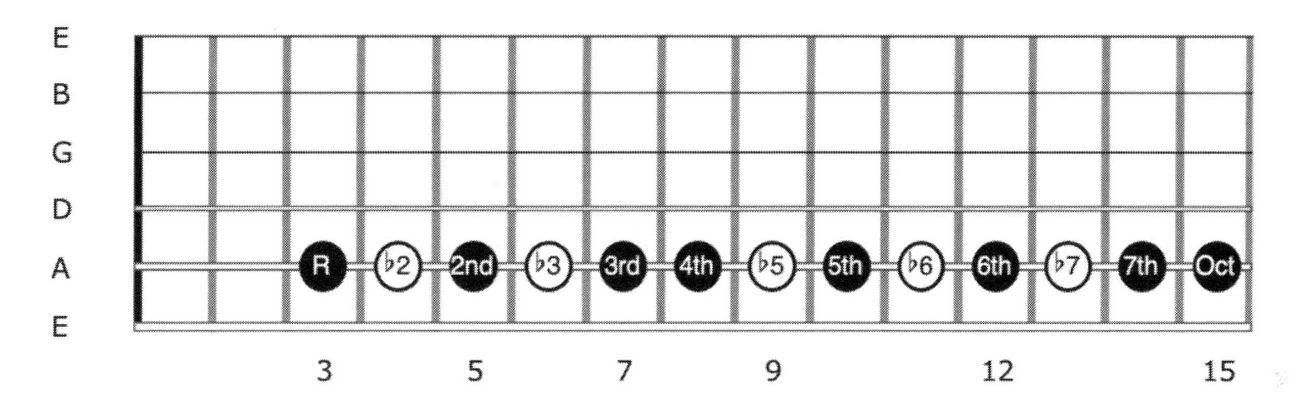

Note that they have only been labelled with one of the possible interval names (more on that in a moment!).

The More 'Traditional' Names

Just like the major scale intervals, chromatic intervals also have more 'traditional' labels which you'll sometimes hear people talk about. It's good to know about these as well.

All the flattened intervals **apart from the *b*5th** are described as being ***minor***.

So, we get a *minor 2nd (b2nd), minor 3rd (b3rd), minor 6th (b6th), minor 7th (b7th).*

The ***b*5th** is described as ***diminished***. So, the traditional name for a *b*5th is a ***diminished 5th***.

When we sharpen an interval, it becomes ***augmented***.

The most common **augmented** interval people talk about is the *augmented 5th (#5th).* You might also hear augmented 4ths or augmented 2nds mentioned from time to time.

And that's pretty much all you need to know about chromatic intervals.

Now, you might be wondering...

Why do some of these intervals have two names? For example, isn't a #2nd (D#) the same as a b3rd (Eb)?

Well spotted!

Often an interval can be described using more than one name. For example, F# is the same note as G*b*. So, both F# or G*b* could be described as the #4th or a *b*5th of C.

Which name is the 'correct' one depends on the context. In the above example, F# should really be called a #4th because F is the 4th and we're sharpening it.

Likewise, G*b* should really be called a *b*5th because G is the 5th and we're flattening it.

You don't need to get too fussy about this sort of thing though, at the end of the day they're just labels. Just make sure you understand the connection between these similar kinds of intervals.

I thought there was no B#, E# or Fb....yet sometimes people talk about these notes as intervals. What's going on?

I wasn't going to mention this, but I think it's best to explain it a little in case you ever encounter it!

The 5th of an A major scale is E. So, in some cases people might describe a #5th as the note E#, even though this note doesn't really exist and is actually F!

The 3rd of the A*b* major scale is C. So, you could hear the *b*3rd called C*b* (actually B).

None of this is that important so don't let this confuse you. It's simply one of those music theory protocols you'll come across from time to time.

Are these interval names linked to the names that we give chords?

Absolutely!

Remember how the minor triad contained a *b*3rd?

Well now you know that the proper name for a *b*3rd is a *minor* 3rd. This helps explain why the triad is named the way it is.

If you come across an *augmented* chord or a *diminished* chord you can be pretty certain that they contain an augmented or diminished 5th in there somewhere!

That's most of what you need to know about chromatic intervals...

Hopefully you can now see that chromatic intervals aren't nearly as scary as they sound!

In fact, they're pretty easy when you understand how the major scale intervals work.

You now have what you need to gain a pretty thorough understanding of intervals, so go back over this chapter and double check everything is crystal clear. Make sure to learn the chromatic intervals as both numbers and the more traditional 'classical' names (you'll encounter them both!).

We'll be continuing our studies of intervals in the second book in this series when we'll examine compound intervals.

Test yourself using the questions that follow and when you're ready I'll see you in the next chapter where we're going to start looking at major keys (a super important topic!).

So good luck with this chapter and see you in the next one!

<u>Now, Test Yourself on Chromatic Intervals!</u>

A **chromatic interval** is a major scale interval which has been ______________________ or ______________________.

The notes in the D major scale are:

D E F# G A B C#

What is the *b*3rd of D? ______________

What is the *b*7th of D? ______________

What is the #5th of D? ______________

What is the *b*6th of D? ______________

What is the #2nd of D? ______________

What is the *b*5th of D? ______________

What is the *b*2nd of D? ______________

What is the #4th of D? ______________

The notes in the A major scale are:

A B C# D E F# G#

Provide the *'traditional'* names for the following intervals.

A to B*b* is the interval of a ______________________.

A to G is the interval of a ___________________________.

A to C is the interval of a ___________________________.

A to E*b* is the interval of a ___________________________.

A to D# is the interval of a ___________________________.

A to F is the interval of a ___________________________.

A to E# is the interval of a ___________________________.

Find out how you did by checking the answers on the next page!

Find Out How You Did!

*A **chromatic interval** is a major scale interval which has been sharpened or flattened.*

The notes in the D major scale are:

D E F# G A B C#

The b3rd of D is F.

The b7th of D is C.

The #5th of D is A#.

The b6th of D is Bb.

The #2nd of D is E# (see lesson notes if this is confusing!).

The b5th of D is Ab.

The b2nd of D is Eb.

The #4th of D is G#.

The notes in the A major scale are:

A B C# D E F# G#

***A to Bb** is a minor 2nd.*

***A to G** is a minor 7th.*

***A to C** is a minor 3rd.*

***A to Eb** is a diminished 5th.*

***A to D#** is an augmented 4th.*

***A to F** is a minor 6th.*

***A to E#** is an augmented 5th.*

Chapter 7: Major Keys (Part 1)

You're nearly halfway through this book - great work!

I hope you're finding these lessons are helping to blow away some of the confusion and misunderstanding which seems to plague guitar players when it comes to music theory!

So far, we've looked at intervals, triads, what the major scale is and more.

Now it's time to use some of this knowledge to examine one of the most important music theory topics there is: keys.

Musicians talk about 'keys' a lot, but I've found many of them don't really understand what a key actually is!

It's a big subject, so we're going to break it down into two separate chapters to make it more manageable and less overwhelming.

We're going to focus only on major keys for the time being. Minor keys are coming later and are much easier to understand when you know about major keys.

In this chapter we're going to take a big picture view of what a major key is.

Then in the follow up chapter we'll dig in a bit deeper and complete your understanding.

Let's get started!

Major Keys: the 'Big Picture' View

Musicians often talk about ***keys***, for example:

Musician 1: Hey, can you tell me what key you play this song in?

Musician 2: Sure, it's in F major

But what do they actually mean?

I like to use this simple definition of a key:

The 'key' a song is in tells you what scale the 'raw material' used in the song comes from

We could define 'raw material' as the notes making up any riffs or licks, the notes the singer uses to sing a melody and the notes in the chords played in the song's chord sequence; basically, all the musical 'building blocks' used to create the song.

So, when the musician in the conversation above says the 'song is in the key of F major', he means:

All the notes sung in the melody of this song...

All the notes in any solos that are played...

All the notes contained in the chords that make up the chord sequence...

All the notes in the bass line of the song...

And pretty much everything else in the song...

All use the seven notes in the F major scale.

The F major scale is like the 'source' of everything in the song.

Make sense?

In a nutshell, that's what a key is. It does get a little more complicated than this in practice, but for now stick with this simple explanation, it'll help keep things from being confusing.

One of the greatest benefits of understanding how a key works is that you can suddenly make sense of chord sequences and songs like never before!

Let's take a look at how chords and keys relate to each other without getting too deep into the theory. We'll be covering that in the next chapter.

Chord Families

We know that the major scale contains seven notes. What's really cool is that we can do something with these seven notes to make **seven chords**.

This means you no longer just have a scale pattern or series of single notes, you now have a 'family' of seven chords which can be combined to create songs and chord sequences of your very own.

To emphasise this 'family' idea even more, the scale the chords come from is often referred to as the ***'parent scale'***.

For example, in the key of G major we have these seven chords:

G	Am	Bm	C	D	Em	F# diminished

Don't worry too much about *why* these are the chords in the key of G, we'll be looking at that in the next chapter. Just know that these chords can be traced back to the notes in the G major scale. The G major scale is the *parent scale*.

As these chords are all in the same 'chord family' and come from the same parent scale, they will all sound 'good' together when we mix them up.

When most people write a song, they're not just sticking chords together randomly. They know what key their song is in and which chords are in the chord family for that key. Using these chords, they can then construct a chord sequence for their song.

It could be:

G	D	Em	C	G	D	C	G

(Play this using any chord shapes you know to hear how it sounds!)

Alternatively, our imaginary composer might try a different chord sequence:

G	Am	C	D	Em	C	D	D

(Play this one and hear the sound!)

There are hundreds more possible chord combinations and which one is used is up to the composer.

Hopefully what we've just discussed has removed some of the mystery surrounding the subject of how to write a song or a chord sequence!

That's Chords: What About the Parent Scale?

Understanding keys means you can write melodies or 'tunes' over chord sequences. To do this use the notes in the parent major scale.

Let's go back to the chord sequences we looked at a moment ago in the key of G major.

The chords in the chord sequences came from the notes in the G major scale (the parent scale). So, we can use the notes in the G major scale to compose melodies, licks or riffs over them.

What we do with these notes is up to us. The notes in the scale are just the 'tools' for writing melody. We need to use these tools creatively to make interesting music but, generally speaking, all the notes will 'fit' with the chords.

Now, you might be wondering...

How many different major keys are there?

Because there are 12 major scales, there are 12 possible major keys. Each one has its own unique chord family containing seven chords. You can see the chords in each key in the following image. Notice they're numbered 1-7 with Roman numerals. Don't worry about this, we'll be examining it later on.

KEY	I	II	III	IV	V	VI	VII
C	C	Dm	Em	F	G	Am	Bdim
F	F	Gm	Am	B*b*	C	Dm	Edim
B*b*	B*b*	Cm	Dm	E*b*	F	Gm	Adim
E*b*	E*b*	Fm	Gm	A*b*	B*b*	Cm	Ddim
A*b*	A*b*	B*b*m	Cm	D*b*	E*b*	Fm	Gdim
D*b*	D*b*	E*b*m	Fm	G*b*	A*b*	B*b*m	Cdim
G*b*	G*b*	A*b*m	B*b*m	C*b*	D*b*	E*b*m	Fdim
B	B	C#m	D#m	E	F#	G#m	A#dim
E	E	F#m	G#m	A	B	C#m	D#dim
A	A	Bm	C#m	D	E	F#m	G#dim
D	D	Em	F#m	G	A	Bm	C#dim
G	G	Am	Bm	C	D	Em	F#dim

You don't need to learn all the chords in each family right now, but do study a few families a little to help you see how keys work.

Can a song use a chord that isn't in the chord family?

Yes, this does often happen. Sometimes it sounds more interesting to take a 'detour' outside of the key to get a different sound. Don't worry about this too much for now, we'll see how this works in ***Music Theory for Guitarists, Volume 3***. For now, just stick with the simple idea presented here in this chapter. The more complex material can wait for the time being.

What about soloing and improvisation on guitar?

Understanding keys can help you make big breakthroughs in your soloing.

When you are able to analyse a chord sequence and work out which key it is in, you can make a good decision about which scale to use to improvise over it.

If you can spot that a chord sequence is using the chords in the key of D major, then you know to improvise over them using the D major scale.

You could also use major pentatonic scales instead of the major scale. This will work because the major pentatonic scale is simply a major scale with a few notes left out. Pentatonic scales will be covered in detail in a later chapter.

Try This Practical Exercise:

1. Choose a key on the chord/key chart
2. Take some of the chords in that key and play them together (ignore the diminished chord for the time being)
3. Hear how they 'fit' together well. This is because they're all in the same chord family
4. Try putting them in different orders to create a simple chord sequence which sounds good to you
5. Try some different combinations...just experiment!

Doing this will help you see how useful your new understanding of keys can be!

And that's most of what you need to know to have a basic understanding of major keys ...

Study everything in this chapter. Having a 'big picture' understanding of what a key is will make the theory coming up in the next chapter *way* easier to understand.

Also, remember to test yourself using the questions that follow and check the answers to make sure you understand everything fully.

When you're ready I'll see you in the next chapter where we're going to break down the idea of a key and look at where this family of seven chords actually comes from.

Good luck and see you in the next chapter!

Now, Test Yourself on Major Keys!

What key a song is in tells you what _______________ the 'raw material' used in the song comes from.

If a song is in the key of A major then all the notes making up the melody, the bassline and the notes making up the chords played will be contained in the __________________ scale.

There are _________ major keys in total.

Each key has a 'chord family' containing _____________ chords.

The scale these chords come from is often called the _______________________.

Find out how you did by checking the answers on the next page!

Find Out How You Did!

What key a song is in tells you what **scale** *the 'raw material' used in the song comes from.*

If a song is in the key of A major then all the notes making up the melody, bassline and the notes making up the chords played will be contained in the ***A major*** *scale.*

There are **12** *major keys.*

Each key has a 'chord family' containing **seven** *chords.*

The scale these chords come from is often called the ***parent scale****.*

Chapter 8: Major Keys (Part 2)

In the last chapter we took a big picture view of major keys.

We had this simple definition of a key:

The 'key' a song is in tells you what scale the 'raw material' used in the song comes from

So, if you had a song in the key of C major:

Any riffs or licks, the melody of the song, the chords played in the song's chord sequence, the bassline and anything else would be using only the 7 notes found in the C major scale.

You also saw how each key has a 'chord family' of seven chords for composing chord sequences in that key and how the 'parent scale' can be used to play melodies over these chords.

Now it's time to look at the theory behind this concept and discover where chord families actually come from. This will give you a thorough understanding of major keys.

Tip: If you want to play some of the examples shown but are unsure of the chord shapes, see the ***Useful Chord Shapes*** section of this book.

There's quite a lot in this chapter, but it's super important stuff. So, make yourself comfortable and let's get started.

Building Chord Families from Major Scales

We're going to use the C major scale for this lesson and I'll show you how we create the C major 'chord family'.

I'll take you step by step through the process of building a chord family. By the end of this lesson, you'll understand something which confuses many guitarists for years!

Before we start...

Back in Chapter 4 we 'stacked' the notes in the scale to build major and minor triads. We're going to be using that knowledge now, so if you need a reminder of how it works have a quick re-read of that chapter!

Step 1: Build a triad on the *root* of the scale

Build a triad starting on the root of the C scale: C.

C D **E** F **G** A B

This gives us the notes **C E G**

You can see this is the **Root + 3rd + 5th** of the scale.

Root + 3rd + 5th is the formula for a **major triad**, so the chord is **C** or **C major**.

C is the first chord in the chord family or 'key' of C major.

Step 2: Build a triad on the *2nd* of the scale

Now we're going to do the same thing starting on the next note in the scale. So, we build a triad starting on the 2nd note: **D**.

C **D** E **F** G **A** B

This gives us the notes **D F A.**

To find out what this chord is we need to *compare* it to the notes in the D major scale. Then we can see if it contains a *b*5th, a *b*3rd or whatever and use this information to determine what kind of chord it is.

The D major scale is:

D E F# G A B C#

The notes in a D major triad would be D F# A - but that's **not** what we've got in our triad (D F A). We have an F instead and this is the flattened 3rd of the D scale.

So, our triad is **the Root + *b*3rd + 5th** of the D scale.

Root + *b*3rd + 5th is the formula for a **minor triad**, so the chord is **D minor**

So **Dm is the second chord** in the chord family or 'key' of C major.

Sometimes people find this step a little confusing! If so, go over it a few more times before you move on.

Step 3: Build a triad on the *3rd* of the scale

Now build a triad starting on the 3rd of the scale: **E**.

C D **E** F **G** A **B**

This gives us the notes **E G B.**

To find out what this chord is we need to compare it to the notes in the E major scale. Then we can discover its formula and figure out if it's major, minor, or something else!

The E major scale is:

E F# G# A B C# D#

The notes in an E major triad would be E G# B - but that's **not** what we've got in our triad (E G B). We've got G instead of G# and this is the flattened 3rd of the E scale.

So, our triad is the **Root + *b*3rd + 5th** of the E scale.

Root + *b*3rd + 5th is the formula for a **minor triad**, so the chord is **E minor**

So Em is the third chord in the chord family or 'key' of C major.

So now we have 3 chords in the C major chord family: C, Dm and Em.

Let's carry on building chords from the C major scale.

<u>Step 4: Build a triad on the *4th* of the scale</u>

Now build a triad starting on the 4th of the scale: **F**.

Let's extend the scale into another octave to make it clearer to see:

C D E **F** G **A** B **C** D E F G A B

This gives us the notes **F A C.**

To find out what this chord is we need to compare it to the notes in the F major scale.

The F major scale is:

F G A B*b* C D E

The notes in an F major triad are F A C and that's exactly what we've got in our F triad which came from the C major scale.

So, our triad is the **Root + 3rd + 5th** giving us an **F major** chord.

So, **F is the 4th chord** in the chord family or 'key' of C major.

Step 5: Build a triad on the *5th* of the scale

Now build a triad starting on the 5th of the scale: **G**.

C D E F **G** A **B** C **D** E F G A B C

This gives us the notes **G B D**.

To find out what this chord is we need to compare it to the notes in the G major scale.

The G major scale is:

G A B C D E F#

The notes in a G major triad are G B D, exactly the same as in the G triad which came from the C major scale.

So, our triad is the **Root + 3rd + 5th** of the G scale, giving us a **G major** chord.

G is the 5th chord in the chord family or 'key' of C major.

Step 6: Build a triad on the 6th of the scale

Next build a triad starting on the 6th of the scale: **A**.

C D E F G **A** B **C** D **E** F G A B

This gives us the notes **A C E.**

As before, we must compare it to the notes in the A major scale to figure out what kind of chord it is.

The A major scale is:

A B C# D E F# G#

The notes in an A major triad would be A C# E - **not** what we've got in our triad (A C E). We've got C instead of C#.

C is the flattened 3rd of the A scale.

So, our triad is the **Root + *b*3rd + 5th** of the A scale.

This is the formula for **a minor triad**, making the chord **A minor**.

So **Am is the 6th chord** in the chord family or 'key' of C major.

Step 7: Build a triad on the 7th of the scale

Finally, we build a triad starting on the 7th of the scale: B.

C D E F G A **B** C **D** E **F** G A B

This gives us the notes **B D F.**

As before, compare it to the notes in the B major scale to figure out what kind of chord it is.

The B major scale is:

B C# D# E F# G# A#

The notes in a B major triad would be B D# F# - **not** what we've got in our triad (B D F).

We've got a flattened 3rd (D), but we've also got a *flattened 5th* (F)!

So, our triad is the **Root + *b*3rd + *b*5th** of the B scale.

We haven't seen this kind of triad yet, but **Root + *b*3rd + *b*5th** is the formula for a **diminished triad**.

So, **B diminished is the 7th chord** in the chord family or 'key' of C major.

Diminished triads aren't used that much in most music, but at least now you know what they are.

The Story So Far...

Ok, you can see that by building a triad starting on each note of the C major scale we get a set of 7 chords.

These chords are the 'chord family' which comes from the C major scale.

The process we've just seen is where chord families actually come from.

Let's carry on...

Now Add Roman Numerals...

Let's take the chords in the C major chord family and number them 1-7 with *Roman numerals*.

This gives us:

I	II	III	IV	V	VI	VII
1	2	3	4	5	6	7
C	Dm	Em	F	G	Am	Bdim

(**Note:** The 'normal' numbers are shown too in case you're not familiar with Roman numerals! But numbering with Roman numerals is how this is normally done)

These are the **'chords in the key of C'**.

But now we can now describe each chord using the Roman numeral assigned to it.

E minor is chord **III** ('chord three').

G major is chord **V** ('chord five').

And so on...

If all this Roman numerals stuff seems a bit outdated or strange, stick with me because this is where things start to get exciting!

The 'Magic Formula' For Getting *All* the Chords in *Any* Key!

Imagine if you could instantly recall what all the chords were in every single key...

It'd be amazing huh?

Well, the good news is that with what you've learned so far in this chapter you can easily learn to do exactly that!

Let's take the lessons learned from the C major scale and see how it can be easily applied to all the major scales to get all the chords in every key (it's much easier than you think!).

We need to look at the 'type' of chord we get on each note. This could also be called the 'quality' of the chord (i.e. whether it's major, minor or diminished).

If we look at the chords in the key of C, we can see how **I, IV** and **V** are **major**:

I	II	III	IV	V	VI	VI
MAJOR	MINOR	MINOR	MAJOR	MAJOR	MINOR	DIMINISHED

II, III and **VI** are **minor**:

I	II	III	IV	V	VI	VII
MAJOR	MINOR	MINOR	MAJOR	MAJOR	MINOR	DIMINISHED

Chord VII is **diminished**:

I	II	III	IV	V	VI	VII
MAJOR	MINOR	MINOR	MAJOR	MAJOR	MINOR	DIMINISHED

This could be shown like this:

I	II	III	IV	V	VI	VII
MAJOR	MINOR	MINOR	MAJOR	MAJOR	MINOR	DIMINISHED

Now for the super important bit!

This 'recipe' can be applied to any of the other major scales to get the chords in that key too.

Let's look at how this works.

Look at the 'pattern' of chord types in the table above.

When we superimpose this 'pattern' on top of the notes in any other major scale it instantly tells us the chords in that key as well! All you need to know are the notes in the major scale in question.

A few examples might be useful here...

Example 1:

The F major scale is:

Root	2nd	3rd	4th	5th	6th	7th
F	G	A	B*b*	C	D	E

Apply the 'recipe' or chord pattern to these notes:

I	II	III	IV	V	VI	VII
MAJOR	MINOR	MINOR	MAJOR	MAJOR	MINOR	DIMINISHED
F	G	A	B*b*	C	D	E

And we get the chord family for the key of F:

I	II	III	IV	V	VI	VII
F	Gm	Am	B*b*	C	Dm	Edim

Example 2:

The A major scale is:

Root	2nd	3rd	4th	5th	6th	7th
A	B	C#	D	E	F#	G#

Apply the 'recipe' or chord pattern to these notes:

I	II	III	IV	V	VI	VII
MAJOR	MINOR	MINOR	MAJOR	MAJOR	MINOR	DIMINISHED
A	B	C#	D	E	F#	G#

And you get the chord family for the key of A major:

I	II	III	IV	V	VI	VII
A	Bm	C#m	D	E	F#m	G#dim

Just to be super clear, this trick works for **every** major scale. So, you can use it to work out the chords in every major key (awesome, eh?).

Even better, I've done the hard work for you!

Look at the **chord/key chart** in the last chapter and you'll see every key clearly laid out in this way.

Take a look and see for yourself.

One last important thing...

Before we leave this topic, I want to briefly mention the ***relative minor***.

Every major key has a closely related minor key, called the ***relative minor***.

To find out the relative minor key look at chord **VI** in any major key chord family.

Here is the chord family for the key of G:

I	II	III	IV	V	VI	VII
G	Am	Bm	C	D	Em	F#dim

You can see that chord VI is Em. This tells us that E minor is the relative minor key of G major.

Don't worry too much about this for now, we'll be examining what it means and how it works in a later chapter.

And it's OK if you don't even know what a 'minor key' is! You'll learn all you need to know before you reach the end of this book.

For now, just remember this simple rule:

Chord VI in any major chord family is the *relative minor*

Now you know what you need to know about major keys and where they come from...

Phew!

That was a pretty jam-packed chapter, so don't worry if you didn't get it all first time. Do take the time to study and digest this material over and over again because it is *invaluable*. I can't overstate how important it is!

It helps you:

- Understand songs and chord sequences...
- Work out how to play other people's songs just by listening...
- Write better music of your own...

- Be able to play a great solo over most songs (on the spot without any preparation!)
- Learn and remember songs more easily
- And *loads* more awesome benefits as well!

So, learn the theory...

Study (maybe even *memorise*) the chord/key chart...

... and then test yourself using the questions that follow.

Any time you invest in really nailing your understanding of keys will pay you back many times over in the future, so dig in and master this crucial topic!

Have fun, take your time and when you're ready I'll see you in the next chapter where we're going to look at how to understand chord sequences a little more. I've got a simple little trick which I know you'll find really useful.

Good luck with this chapter and see you again in the next one.

Now, Test Yourself on Major Keys!

In any major key the 'quality' or type of each chord is as follows:

I is ________________.

II is ________________.

III is ________________.

IV is ________________.

V is ________________.

VI is ________________.

VII is ________________.

The notes in the D major scale are as follows:

D E F# G A B C#

What would the seven chords in the key of D be?
(Hint: major, minor, minor etc)

____

Are the following statements true or false?

In any major key triad chords I, IV and V are major.

In any major key the II, IV and VI triad chords are minor.

Chord VII is a diminished triad.

The formula major, minor, minor, major, major, minor, diminished only works for figuring out the chords in the key of C.

The minor chord which is chord VI is the ____________________.

Find out how you did by checking the answers on the next page!

Find Out How You Did!

*I is **major**.*

*II is **minor**.*

*III is **minor**.*

*IV is **major**.*

*V is **major**.*

*VI is **minor**.*

*VII is **diminished**.*

The chords in the key of D major are:

***D major, E minor, F# minor, G major, A major, B minor, C# diminished**.*

***In any major key triad chords I, IV and V are major**.*

This is correct!

***In any major key the II, IV and VI triad chords are minor**.*

*False! Chord IV is major not minor. Chords **II, III** and **VI** are minor!*

***Chord VII is a diminished triad**.*

True!

***The formula major, minor, minor, major, major, minor, diminished only works for figuring out the chords in the key of C**.*

False! It works for all 12 major scales to give the chords in every major key!

The minor chord which is chord VI is the relative minor.

Chapter 9: Understanding Chord Progressions

In the previous two lessons we looked at the theory behind major keys and chord families.

In this lesson we're going to look at a simple concept which will help you understand *chord sequences.*

A *chord sequence* is simply a set of chords joined up and played together. It's what you play when you play through the chords to a song. A chord sequence is also called a *chord progression*.

What you're going to learn in this chapter will help you write stronger sounding chord sequences more easily, as well as work out and remember the chord sequences used in any songs you want to learn.

If you're a composer or a singer/songwriter this knowledge will be really helpful.

If you're an improviser/soloist it will help you to look at a chord sequence, analyse the key, choose an appropriate scale and be able to improvise fluently over it.

If you understand the chord family concept from the last two lessons then this is going to be easy.

Definitely play these examples on your guitar to hear how they sound. You can either use the chord shapes given or other chord shapes you know.

So, let's get into it!

<u>Roman Numerals: what are they all about?</u>

In the last lesson we numbered the seven chords in the C major chord family with Roman numerals like this:

I	II	III	IV	V	VI	VII
C	Dm	Em	F	G	Am	Bdim

This is very helpful!

It means that we can now describe a chord sequence in the key of C in terms of numbers, based on the Roman numerals used for each chord.

For example, the following chord sequence could be described as a **I IV V** chord sequence:

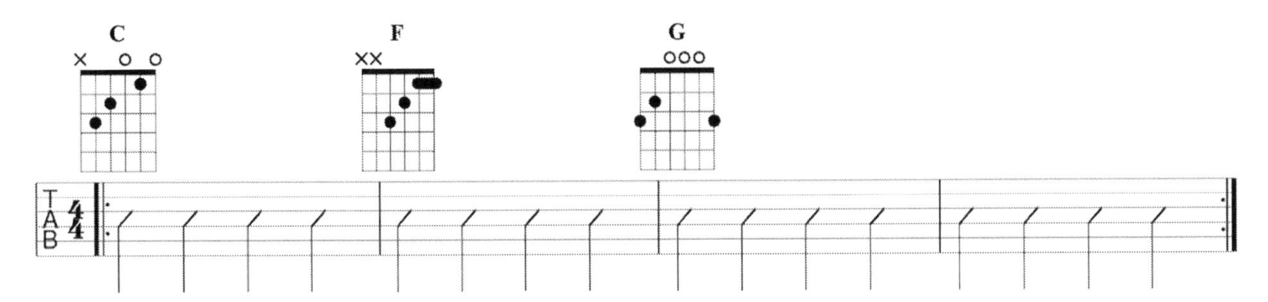

This is because in the C major chord family, C is the **I** chord, F is the **IV** chord and G is the **V** chord:

I	II	III	IV	V	VI	VII
C	Dm	Em	F	G	Am	Bdim

You've probably heard of 'I IV V' chord sequences before, they're one of the most common chord sequences we see in music.

Let's look at a few more examples in the key of C…

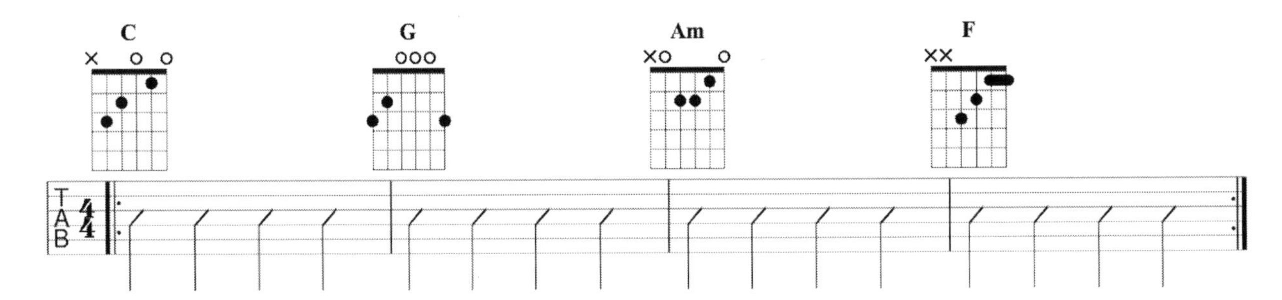

This could be described as a **I V VI IV** chord sequence in the key of C. C is chord **I**, G is chord **V**, A minor is chord **VI** and F is chord **IV**.

I	II	III	IV	V	VI	VII
C	Dm	Em	F	G	Am	Bdim

Here's another example:

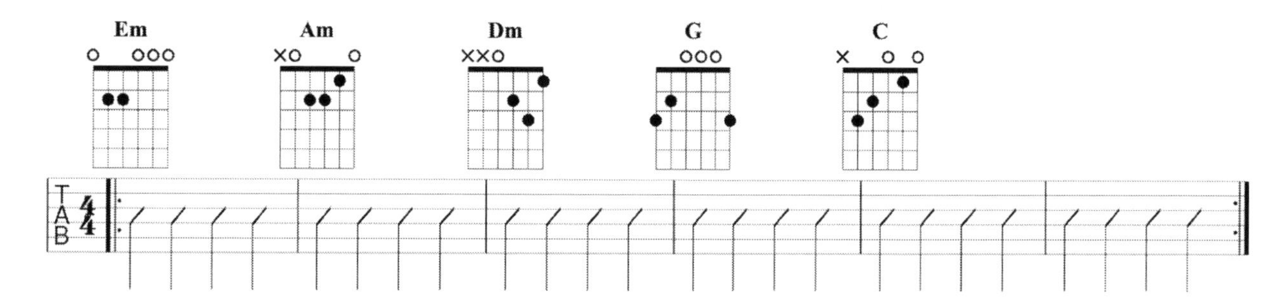

This could be described as a **III VI II V I** chord sequence in the key of C.

I	II	III	IV	V	VI	VII
C	Dm	Em	F	G	Am	Bdim

Understanding this means you can spot what is actually happening in a chord sequence, instead of seeing it as a bunch of random chords joined together. You begin to see chord sequences as logical, step-by-step movements inside a chord family.

Understanding chord progressions also makes it much easier to work out the chord sequence of a song you're trying to learn because you see the same chord sequences used over and over again. With practice you'll almost be able to predict which chord will follow which!

'V to I' or 'Perfect Cadence'

One of the most common things you see in a chord sequence is the **V** chord in a chord family or key, moving or 'resolving' to the **I** chord. In the key of C this would be G (chord V) moving to C (chord I) like in the following chord sequence:

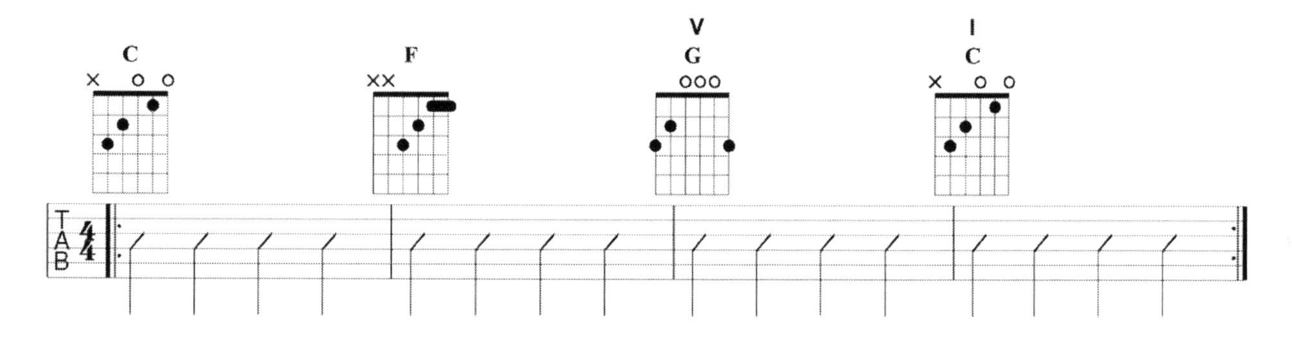

I	II	III	IV	V	VI	VII
C	Dm	Em	F	G	Am	Bdim

This is sometimes called a 'perfect cadence' (a 'cadence' is simply the movement between two chords). Call it this if you like, although I prefer to just think of it as chord **V** going to chord **I**.

Either way, it's probably the most common chord movement there is inside a key, so remember the chord movement **V** to **I** or *perfect cadence*.

Changing Keys Made Easy...

The 'Roman numerals method' is great when you need to move a chord sequence into a different key quickly and easily. This can be really useful if you're working with other musicians.

Imagine you had this chord sequence in the key of G:

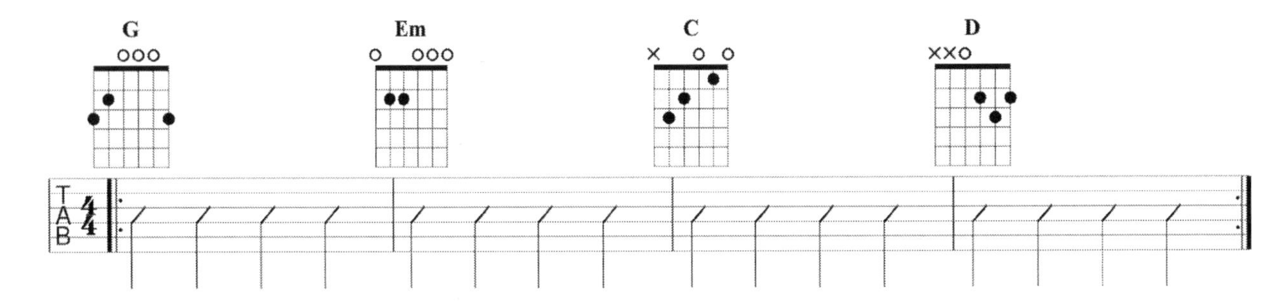

Now let's say you needed to move it into the key of E.

Lots of musicians would panic if they had to do this on the spot! But with the number system we're using here, it's really quite easy.

1. Using the chord/key chart analyse the chord progression in the key of G. You'll see it's a **I, VI, IV, V** progression

I	II	III	IV	V	VI	VII
G	Am	Bm	C	D	Em	F#dim

2. Now look on the chord/key chart and find the **I, VI, IV** and **V** chords in the key of E:

I	II	III	IV	V	VI	VII
E	F#m	G#m	A	B	C#m	D#dim

3. You can see that the **I** chord is E major, C# minor is the **VI** chord, A major is the **IV** chord and **B** major is the **V** chord.

4. Put the chords in the right order, **I VI IV V** and you get the chord sequence moved into the key of E major:

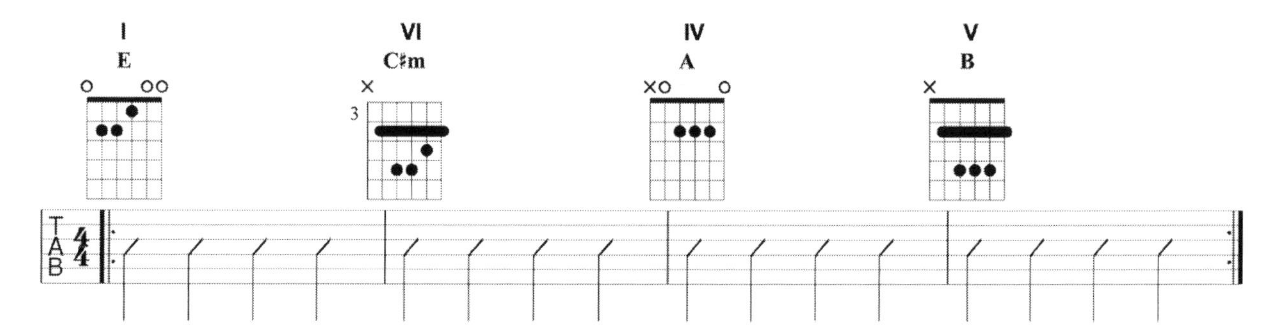

Make sense?

That's most of what you need to know about chord progressions for now...

The subject of chords and chord progressions is a big one and we can't cover *all* of it here. However, if you understand everything in this chapter then you've not only made a great start on it; you also know a lot more about this subject than many other musicians do!

We'll be looking at all sorts of other things to do with chord progressions in books 2 & 3 in this series.

The concepts covered in this chapter are really pretty simple, but it's important to apply them so that they become second nature.

To help you do this, complete the questions coming up next. Fill in the answers to help you see how easy this theory really is!

The questions use common chord sequences which you'll see and hear time and time again in the songs you listen to. You may even recognise them as being used in some songs you know.

You'll find the chord/key chart from Chapter 7 helpful for carrying out this task.

Good luck and when you're ready I'll see you in the next chapter where we're going to be taking a look at pentatonic scales.

Now, Test Yourself on Chord Sequences!

Question 1

Using the chord/key chart to help, write out a **I IV V** chord sequence in the given keys:

Key of **G**: ______________________________________

Key of **F**: ______________________________________

Key of **A**: ______________________________________

Question 2

Using the chord/key chart to help, write out a **I VI II V** chord sequence in the given keys:

Key of **D**: ______________________________________

Key of **E**: ______________________________________

Key of **D*b***: ______________________________________

Question 3

Add Roman numerals to the following chords to describe the chord sequence in the given keys:

Key of **G**:

| G / / / | C / / / | Bm / / / | Am / D / |

Key of **C**:

| C / / / | Am / / / | Dm / / / | G / / / |

Key of **B**:

| G#m / / / | F# / / / | E / / / | B / / / |

Find out how you did by checking the answers on the next page!

Find Out How You Did!

Question 1

I IV V in key of G: ***G C D***

I IV V in key of F: ***F Bb C***

I IV V in key of A: ***A D E***

Question 2

I VI II V in key of D: ***D Bm Em A***

I VI II V in key of E: ***E C#m F#m B***

I VI II V in key of Db: ***Db Bbm Ebm Ab***

Question 3

Add Roman numerals to the following chords to describe the chord sequence in the given keys:

Key of ***G****:*

G///	*C///*	*Bm///*	*Am/*	*D/*
I	***IV***	***III***	***II***	***V***

Key of ***C:***

C///	*Am///*	*Dm///*	*G///*
I	***VI***	***II***	***V***

Key of ***B****:*

G#m///	*F#///*	*E///*	*B///*
VI	***V***	***IV***	***I***

Chapter 10: Pentatonic Scales

It's time to take a break from chords and keys and look at one of *the* most commonly used set of tools employed by guitarists of all styles: **pentatonic scales**.

You're most likely using pentatonic scales already when you play, in fact the *minor pentatonic scale* is probably the first scale you ever learned to play on guitar.

But what are pentatonic scales and how do we use them?

That's what this lesson is all about, so hold on as we take a look at the theory behind these exceptionally useful scales!

What Is a 'Pentatonic' Scale?

A simple definition of a pentatonic scale is:

a 5 note scale

Yes, it really is as simple as that!

'Pent' means *five* (think of pentagon, pentathlon, pentagram etc) and ***'tonic'*** means *note*.

So, any scale containing just 5 notes can be labelled a 'pentatonic scale'.

There are lots of different pentatonic scales, but the two you're most likely to need are the ***minor pentatonic*** and ***major pentatonic*** scales. These are the focus of this chapter.

Let's examine the *major* pentatonic scale first.

What is the Major Pentatonic scale?

The major pentatonic scale is simply the major scale with a few notes removed.

To be more exact, it's a major scale with the **4th** and **7th** notes **taken out**.

Here's a **G major scale**:

G	A	B	C	D	E	F#
1	2	3	4	5	6	7

Leave out the **4th** and **7th** and we get the **G major pentatonic** scale:

G	A	B	D	E
1	2	3	5	6

The major pentatonic scale is a 5 note scale containing the root, 2nd, 3rd, 5th and 6th notes from a major scale.

Let's see how this works on the guitar neck. Here's a common way to play a G major scale around the 3rd fret area of the guitar:

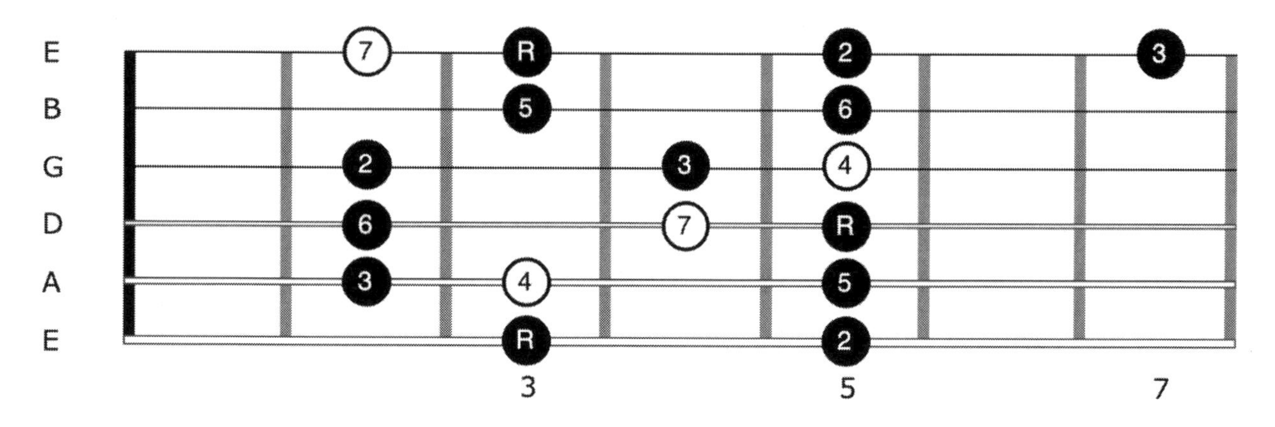

Notice in the diagram above the 4th and 7th are shown as white dots instead of black. Take them out of the scale pattern and you get a common way of playing a G major pentatonic scale:

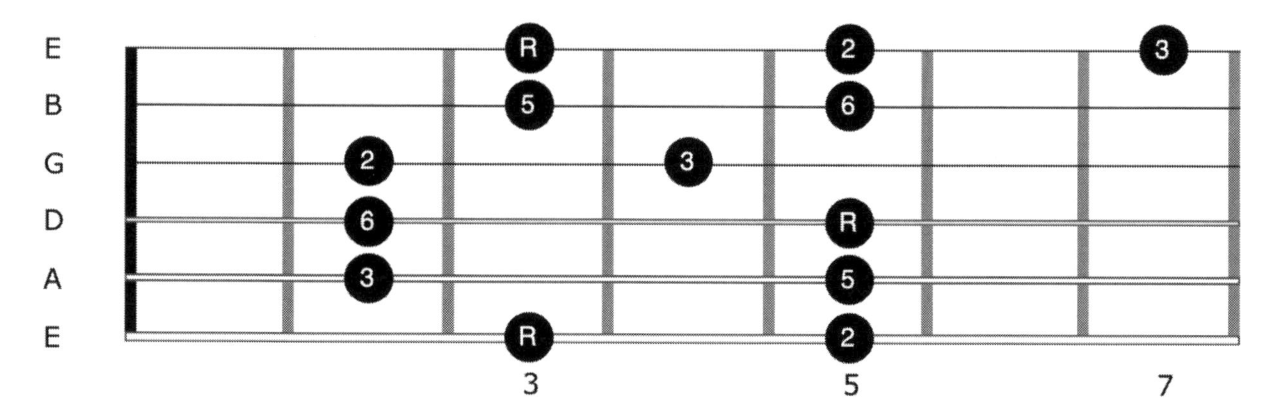

You can see that the scale contains the root, 3rd and 5th from the G major scale (labelled R, 3, 5 on the diagram). In other words, it is built around a G major triad:

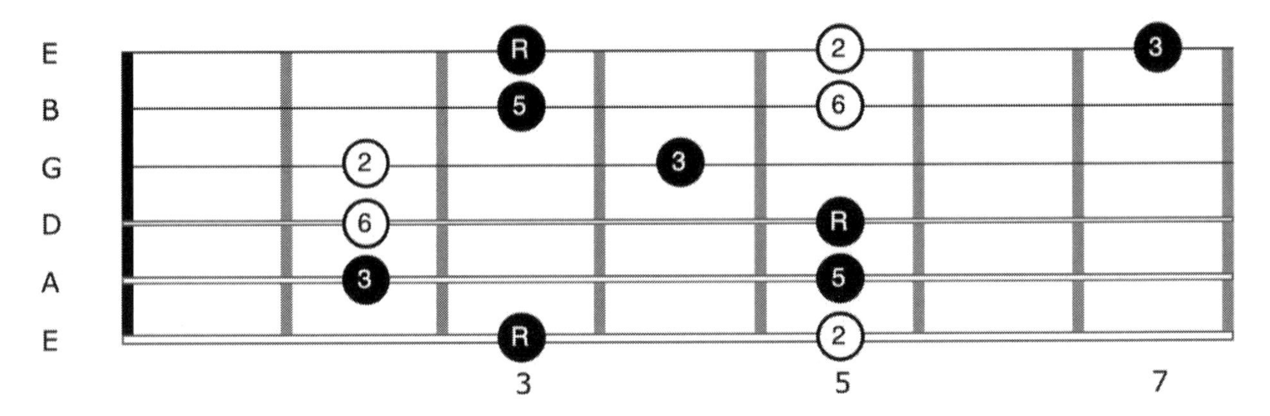

This is what makes this scale **major** instead of minor.

What is the major pentatonic scale used for?

The major pentatonic scale is normally used for playing licks, solos and melodies in a major key. This works because apart from the 4th and 7th being left out, it's the same as a major scale anyway! All the important 'major ingredients' are still in there, making it a great stand in for the major scale in many playing situations.

So, over a chord progression in the key of G major you could solo with the G major pentatonic scale *instead* of the G major scale.

Does it work better than a major scale?

This a matter of opinion, but in many cases I think it does. The reason is that the 4th and 7th notes can sound a little 'weak' in the major scale. This totally depends on the situation they're being played in, but in many cases, people find the major pentatonic a better choice than the major scale when soloing.

Where can I find out more about the major pentatonic scale?

Learning how to use the scale is really beyond the scope of this book, but don't worry, in the ***Useful Resources*** section you'll find links to some of my lessons and courses which do show you how to use this powerful 5 note scale!

What is the Minor Pentatonic scale?

The minor pentatonic scale is a *five note* minor scale. It is built using the **root + *b*3rd + 4th + 5th + *b*7th** from a major scale.

Here's a **G major scale**:

G	A	B	C	D	E	F#
1	2	3	4	5	6	7

Take the **root, *b*3rd, 4th, 5th and *b*7** notes of the scale and you get a **G** minor pentatonic scale:

G	B*b*	C	D	F
1	*b*3rd	4	5	*b*7

Let's see how this works on the guitar neck. Here's the G major scale shape from earlier:

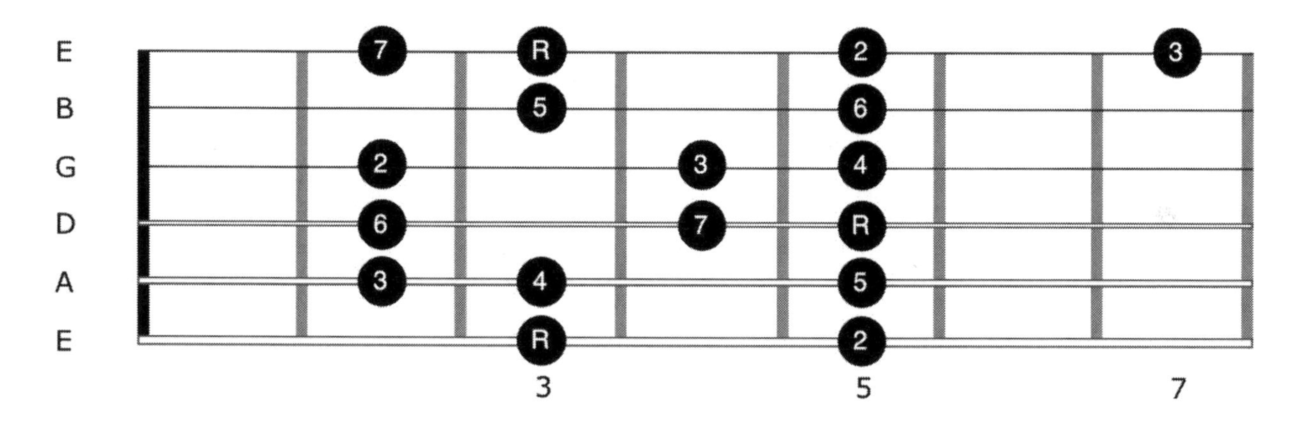

Take out the 2nd and 6th. Then *flatten* the 3rd and the 7th notes. This gives us the most common way of playing the minor pentatonic scale:

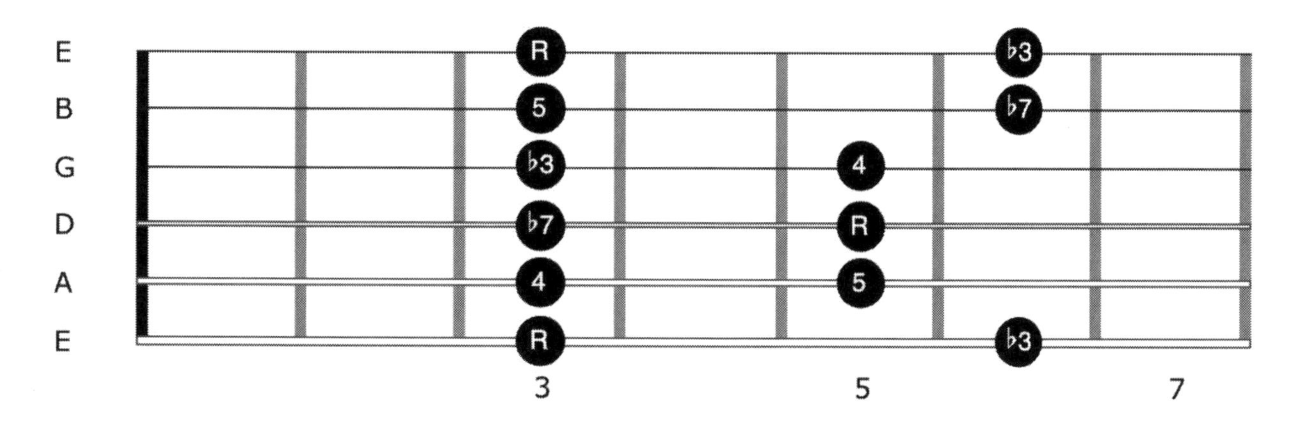

Notice how, for convenience, the *b*3rd has been moved from the A string to the low E string. Also, the b7th on the top E string has been moved onto the B string. Doing this gives a scale fingering which is more practical and easier to use when we play.

You can see that the scale contains the root, *b*3rd and 5th (labelled R, *b*3, 5 on diagram). This is the formula for a *minor triad*.

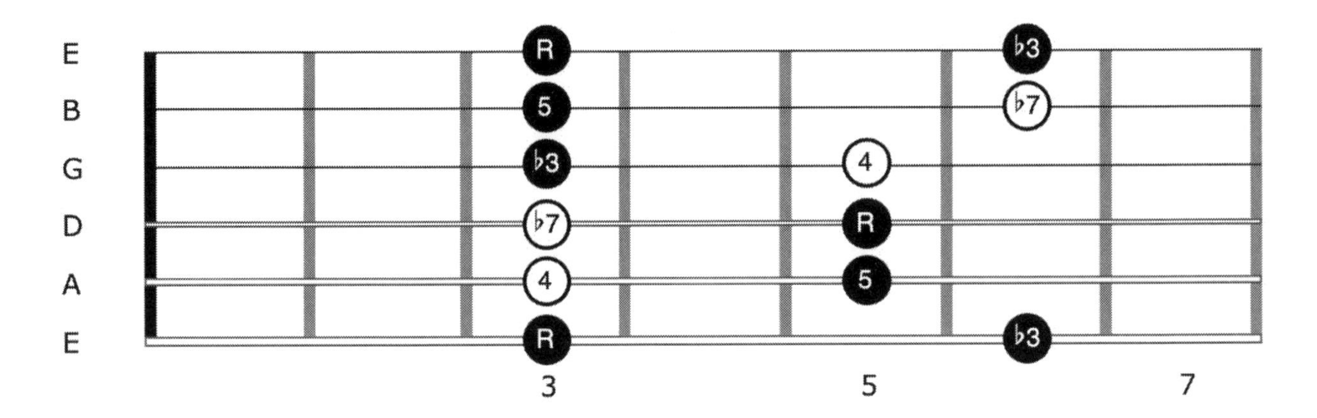

In other words, the G minor pentatonic scale is built on a G minor triad. This is what makes this scale sound *minor* instead of major.

What is the minor pentatonic scale used for?

The minor pentatonic scale is the 'first choice' scale used for playing licks, solos and melodies in a minor key. So much pop and rock music is in minor keys that the minor pentatonic is used most of the time in these styles. If you're unsure about what a 'minor key' is, don't worry, we'll be looking at that soon in an upcoming chapter.

As an example, over a chord progression in the key of D minor you could solo using the D minor pentatonic scale.

It is also the default scale for playing **blues**. Even though we're normally playing over *dominant 7th* chords (like A7, E7 etc) instead of minor chords...the minor pentatonic just 'works' over the whole 12 bar blues.

So, for playing over a 12 bar blues in E you could use the E minor pentatonic scale.

Is the minor pentatonic the same as the blues scale?

The minor pentatonic is very similar to the *blues scale*. The blues scale has an added *b*5th note.

For example, the G minor pentatonic scale is:

G	B*b*	C	D	F
1	*b*3rd	4	5	*b*7

The 5th is D.

Flatten it to D*b*, add it in and you get G blues scale:

G	B*b*	C	D*b*	D	F
1	*b*3rd	4	*b*5	5	*b*7

We can add this *b*5th note to our G minor pentatonic scale shape to get the most common way of playing a G blues scale:

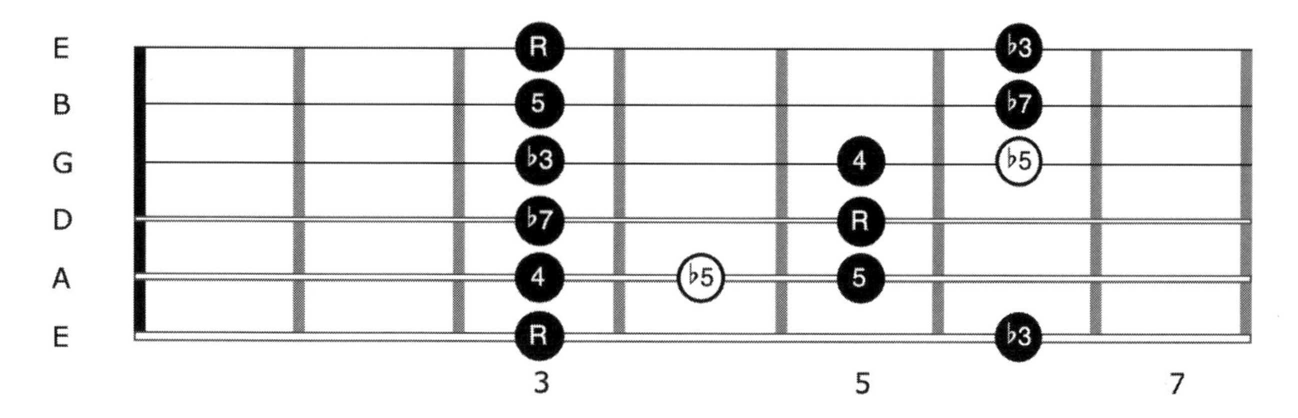

The two scales are often used somewhat interchangeably, especially when playing blues or rock.

Where can I find out more about the minor pentatonic scale?

See the ***Useful Resources*** section at the back of this book to find links to many of my best lessons on the minor pentatonic scale as well as details of my complete ***Minor Pentatonic Mastery*** course!

That's most of what you need to know about pentatonic scale theory for now...

Now you know the theory behind pentatonic scales. As I said earlier, there are other pentatonic scales and other applications for them outside of what we've discussed here, but this will give you a good all round understanding of what pentatonic scales are. If you'd like to know more about the major and minor pentatonic scales and discover an easy way to learn and use them all over the fretboard, then see my ***CAGED System for Guitar*** book.

For now, test yourself with the questions coming up next, and remember to look out for this theory being used in any pentatonic licks or solos you know. Doing this will help you see this theory being used in 'real life' music.

Have fun and see you in the next chapter!

Now, Test Yourself on Pentatonic Scales!

Pentatonic scales contain __________ notes.

The two most common pentatonic scales are the _______________and______________ pentatonic.

The **major pentatonic** is like a major scale but without the ______ and _______ notes.

These are removed. It is built on a ___________ triad and used for playing in __________ keys.

Here is an F major scale:

F G A B*b* C D E

The notes in **F major pentatonic** are _________________________.

When soloing, the major pentatonic scale is commonly used in place of the _________ scale.

The minor pentatonic is a 5 note scale with the formula ______________________________.

It is built on a ___________ triad and used for playing in __________ keys as well as over

____.

Here is a C major scale:

C D E F G A B

The notes in **C minor pentatonic** are _________________________.

The minor pentatonic scale is similar to the blues scale. The only difference is that the blues scale has an added __________.

Find out how you did by checking the answers on the next page!

Find Out How You Did!

*Pentatonic scales contain **5** notes.*

*The two most common pentatonic scales are the **minor** and **major** pentatonic.*

*The major pentatonic is like a major scale but without the **4th** and **7th** notes. These are removed. It is built on a **major** triad and used for playing in **major** keys.*

Here is an F major scale:

F G A Bb C D E

*The notes in F major pentatonic are **F G A C D**.*

*When soloing, the major pentatonic scale is commonly used in place of the **major** scale.*

*The minor pentatonic is a 5 note scale with the formula: **root, b3rd, 4th, 5th, b7th**. It is built on a **minor** triad and used for playing in **minor** keys as well as over a **12 bar blues**.*

Here is a C major scale:

C D E F G A B

*The notes in C minor pentatonic are **C Eb F G Bb**.*

*The minor pentatonic scale is similar to the blues scale. The only difference is that the blues scale has an added **b5th**.*

Chapter 11: The Natural Minor Scale

In this chapter we're going to take a quick look at the **natural minor scale**.

This will help you clearly understand minor keys, which we'll be looking at in the next chapter.

Let's start by examining what the natural minor scale is and how it is different from the major scale.

Here's What You Need To Know About The Natural Minor Scale...

As with the major scale, the ***natural minor scale*** contains 7 notes.

Let's see how it is different to the major scale.

Imagine we had an A major scale. It contains the notes:

A B C# D E F# G#

To change it into the natural minor scale we need to ***flatten*** 3 notes: the **3rd**, the **6th** and the **7th**.

This gives us:

A B C D E F G

Doing this has given us the ***A natural minor scale***.

If we wanted to describe the natural minor scale in terms of its intervals, we could use the following formula or recipe:

R 2nd *b*3rd 4th 5th *b*6th *b*7th

Notice it has a *minor third* (*b*3rd). Remember, this is *the* note that makes it a minor scale as opposed to a major type scale.

Let's look at another example. Here is the E major scale:

E F# G# A B C# D#

Flatten the **3rd, 6th** and **7th** and the result is the ***E natural minor scale***:

E F# G A B C D

So now you know about the structure of the natural minor scale and how it differs from the major scale.

Here is a common way of playing the natural minor scale on the guitar. The A natural minor scale is shown in this example:

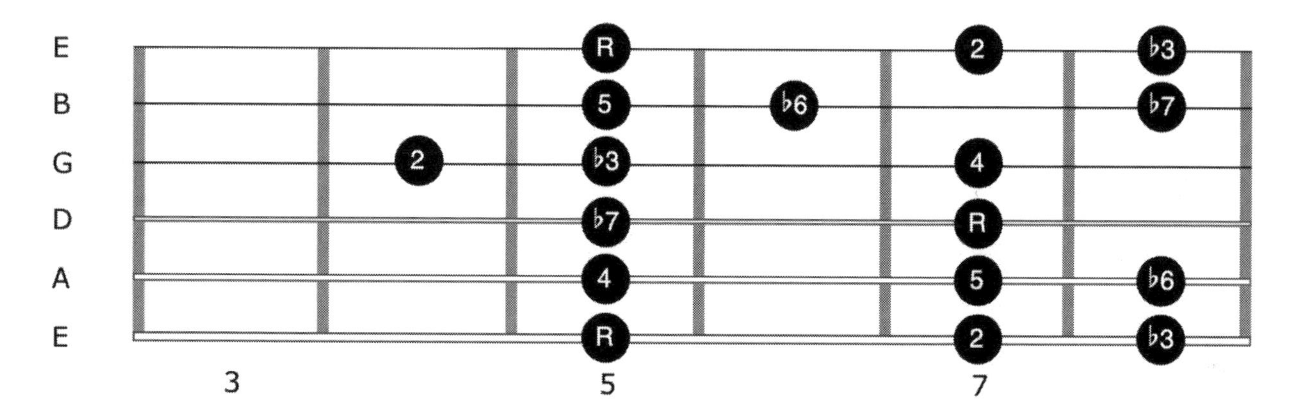

Look very carefully at this scale shape. You might be able to spot the minor pentatonic scale shape hiding inside the pattern.

Here's the natural minor scale again. The minor pentatonic scale is shown in black. See it now?

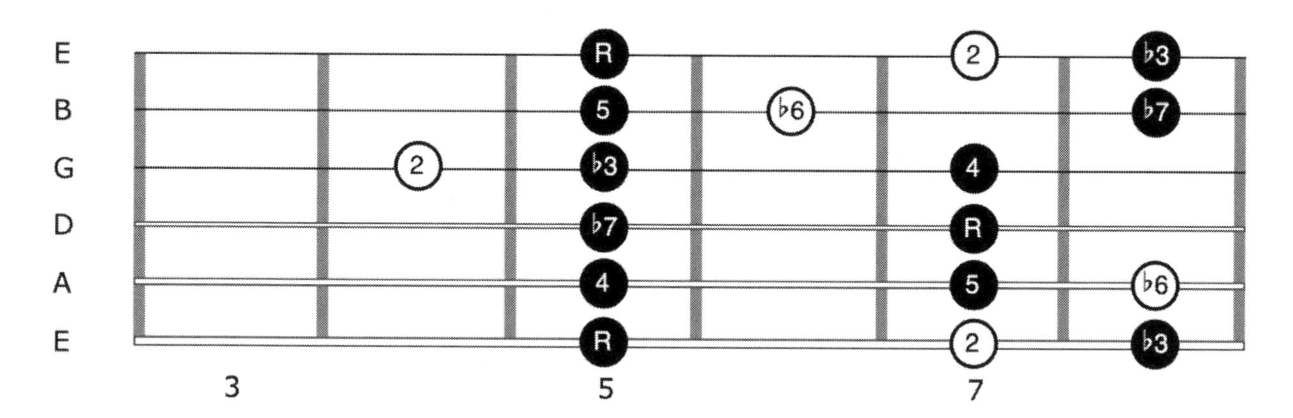

This gives us some other ways of describing the minor pentatonic scale.

For example, we could think of it as the natural minor scale *without* the 2nd and *b*6th.

Or, as the *root, b3rd, 4th, 5th* and *b7th* notes from the natural minor scale.

This minor pentatonic 'framework' is a great help in learning how to use the natural minor scale when we play. We can take our minor pentatonic licks and ideas and continue to use them, perhaps adding in the 2nd and *b*6th for some natural minor 'flavour' as well.

This topic is beyond the scope of this book. See my ***CAGED System for Guitar*** book for much more on the natural minor scale including scale patterns, sample licks and tips for using it in your playing.

Now, you might be wondering...

Why do I need to know about the natural minor scale?

This is a good question. I haven't yet shown you *why* you need to know all this!

The aim of this chapter is just to *introduce* you to the natural minor scale and explain what it is. In the next chapter we'll be getting into why it's important and what you can use it for when you make music.

Does the natural minor scale have any other names?

Yes. You'll also hear this scale called the *Aeolian mode*. There is a reason for this, but we don't need to worry about it right now!

And that's *most* of what you need to know about the natural minor scale (until the next chapter!)

But we'll be seeing it again in the next chapter where you'll learn about some of the important uses for the scale and why it's a good idea to understand it.

Test yourself with the questions coming up next and apply the practical exercises to help you get familiar with this important scale.

When you're ready I'll see you in the next chapter where we're going to be getting stuck into the theory behind **minor keys**!

Now, Test Yourself on the Natural Minor Scale!

The natural minor scale contains __________ notes.

Complete the interval formula for the natural minor scale:

Root - 2nd ____- ____- ____- ____- ____

The specific note or interval which makes the natural minor a minor type scale is the _____________.

This is also known as the _______________.

Here are the notes in the C major scale:

C D E F G A B

Write out the notes in the **C natural minor** scale:

____

The natural minor scale is sometimes called the ____________________.

We can find a ___________________ scale hiding inside the natural minor scale.

Find out how you did by checking the answers on the next page!

Find Out How You Did!

*The natural minor scale contains **7** notes.*

The interval formula for the natural minor scale is:

Root - 2nd b3rd 4th 5th b6th b7th

*The specific note or interval which makes the natural minor a minor type scale is the **b3rd**. This is also known as the **minor third**.*

The notes in the C natural minor scale are:

C D Eb F G Ab Bb

*The natural minor is sometimes called the **Aeolian mode**.*

*We can find a **minor pentatonic** scale hiding inside the natural minor scale.*

Chapter 12: Minor Key Basics

In Chapters 7 and 8 you learned about major keys.

But here's the thing: lots of music is not in a major key. Instead, it's in what is called a *minor key*.

So, in this chapter we're going to examine minor keys. We'll see what they are, where they come from and how to use them when you make music.

Tip: If you want to play some of the examples shown but are unsure of the chord shapes, see the ***Useful Chord Shapes*** section of this book.

Let's get started!

What Is a Minor Key (The 'Big Picture View')?

Let's start by hearing the difference in sound between a major and a minor key. If you've got a guitar handy, play this chord sequence in the key of D major:

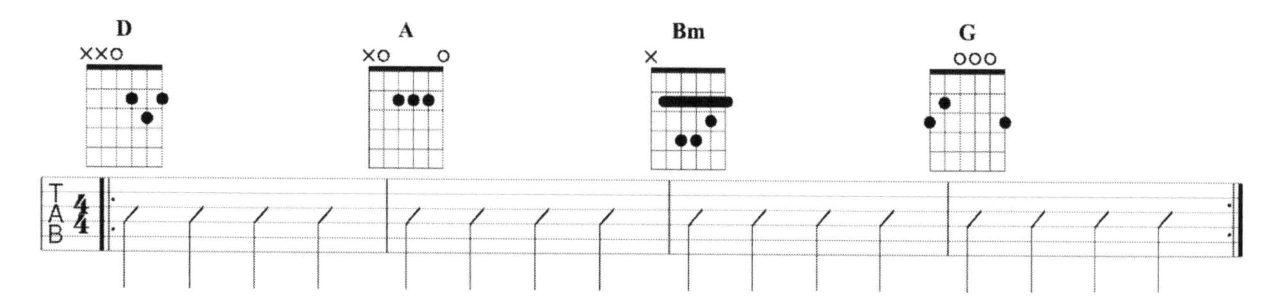

Now play through this one in the key of D minor:

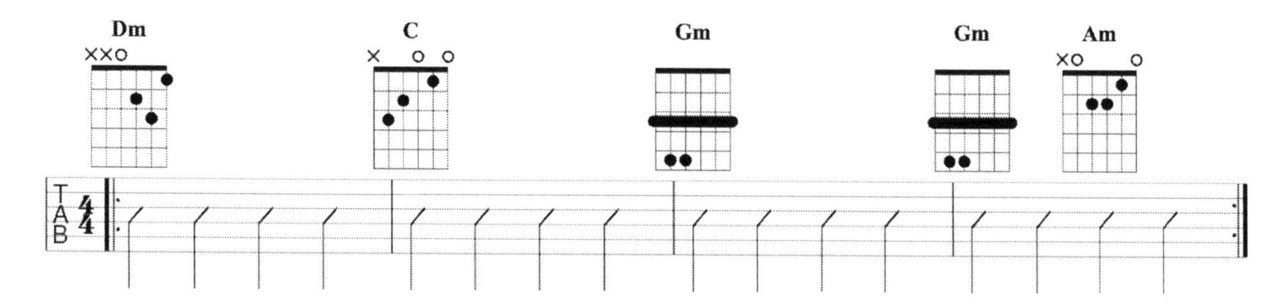

Notice how the minor key gives us a 'darker' or 'sadder' sound and mood.

To put it *very* simply:

Music in a major key sounds *bright, happy* and *uplifting*

Music in a minor key sounds *darker, sadder* and more *'gloomy'*

Both the above statements are *vast* simplifications! But they're helpful for learning the difference in the sound between the two types of keys.

Songwriters will choose a major or minor key depending on the mood and feel they want to create and the effect they want it to have on the listener.

How do we know what chords to use for music in minor keys?

Simple; minor key chord families!

Minor Key Chord Families

Just like major keys, each minor key has a chord family of 7 chords.

Here's a quick reminder of what we did in **Chapter 8** to create 12 major keys:

1. We stacked major scale notes on top of each other to create 7 triads. We called this a 'chord family'
2. We referred to the scale the chord family came from as the 'parent scale'.
3. We described the scale and the chord family together as a 'key'
4. We saw how we can use the scale and chords together to write and play music in that key

Minor keys and minor chord families come from doing this exact same process to the **natural minor scale** we saw in the last chapter!

In other words, if we take a G natural minor scale and build triads on each note, we can use the chords in the resulting chord family to create chord progressions in the key of G minor.

Then we can use the notes in the G natural minor scale to craft melodies, licks, riffs and anything else you can think of over the top.

Basically, this is how minor keys work.

The 'Relative Minor Shortcut'

You might be thinking 'Great, now I've got to learn *all the chords* in *all* the minor chord families *as well as* the major ones!'

Well, hold on...

We saw the *relative minor* 'rule' at the end of Chapter 8:

Chord VI in any major chord family is the *relative minor*

Here is where this helps us out:

The 7 chords in the chord family for any major key and its relative minor key are exactly the same.

Let's back this up with a quick example. Here are the chords in the key of G major:

I	II	III	IV	V	VI	VII
G	Am	Bm	C	D	Em	F#dim

The relative minor key of G major is Em. The chords in the E minor chord family are:

I	II	III	IV	V	VI	VII
Em	F#dim	G	Am	Bm	C	D

You can see that they are exactly the same chords in the same order, but starting on chord **VI**. We've labelled Em the **I** chord because we are thinking of the chords as now being in the key of E minor *not* G major.

This makes things much simpler. We just need to take all 12 major key chord families, keep the chords in the same order but and make each VI chord into the I chord.

Then we have all 12 minor key chord families!

Here are the chords in the 12 minor key chord families, organised with the 'most common' minor keys first:

KEY	I	II	III	IV	V	VI	VII
A minor	Am	Bdim	C	Dm	Em	F	G
E minor	Em	F#dim	G	Am	Bm	C	D
D minor	Dm	Edim	F	Gm	Am	Bb	C
G minor	Gm	Adim	Bb	Cm	Dm	Eb	F
B minor	Bm	C#dim	D	Em	F#m	G	A
C minor	Cm	Ddim	Eb	Fm	Gm	Ab	Bb
F minor	Fm	Gdim	Ab	Bbm	Cm	Dd	Eb
F# minor	F#m	G#dim	A	Bm	C#m	D	E
C# minor	C#m	D#dim	E	F#m	G#m	A	B
Bb minor	Bbm	Cdim	Db	Ebm	Fm	Gb	Ab
Eb minor	Ebm	Fdim	Gb	Abm	Bbm	Cb	Db
G# minor	G#m	A#dim	B	C#m	D#m	E	F#

If you look at chord III you can see the major key that each minor key is the relative minor to. You can think of this as the 'relative major' key.

Warning: Lots of people get confused and wonder ...

If the chords in a major key and a relative minor key are basically the same...then what's the difference? And why don't chord sequences in the two keys sound exactly the same?

The answer is all to do with which chord is 'emphasised', or made to sound like the '*main chord*'.

Let's look at an example.

The key of C major has the same chord family as the key of A minor (its relative minor key).

Say we had the following four chords from the chord family:

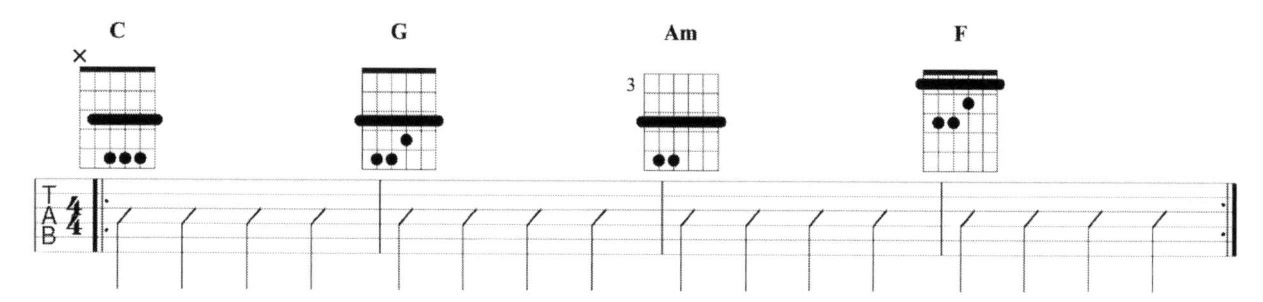

Play this example and you'll hear how it sounds 'happy' like it's in the key of C major. This is because we have 'framed' C major so it sounds like the 'main chord' in the sequence.

How about we change the order of the chords:

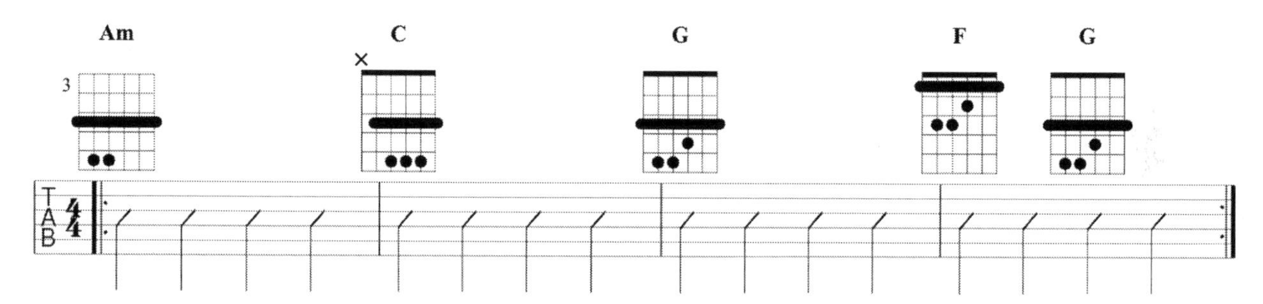

Play this example and you'll hear that A minor now sounds like the 'main chord'. This gives the chord sequence the 'sadder' sound of a minor key chord progression.

So, although the chords in each key are the same, putting them in different orders can create both major key and minor key chord progressions that will sound good.

Often, but not always the first chord in a progression gives you a clue about which key the progression is in (like in the examples above). Use this to help you, but remember it doesn't *always* work like this!

Common Minor Key Chord Progressions

Just like with major keys, in minor keys there are common chord progressions which are used a lot.

Here's the chord family in the key of E minor:

I	II	III	IV	V	VI	VII
Em	F#dim	G	Am	Bm	C	D

Chord I is often used with chords **VI** and **VII** to create strong sounding chord progressions.

Here are two examples. Play them and see what they sound like:

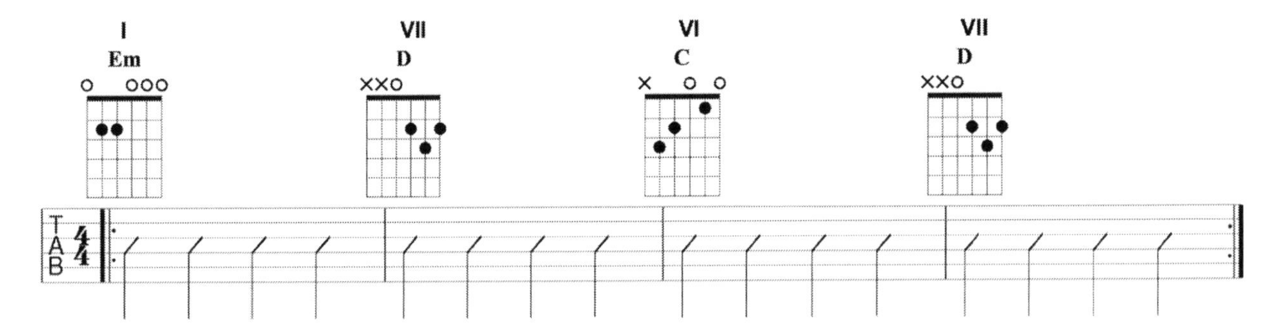

We could think of this as **I-VII-VI-VII** in the key of E minor.

If we change the order around, we get another common sequence. This could be called a **I-VI-VII** progression:

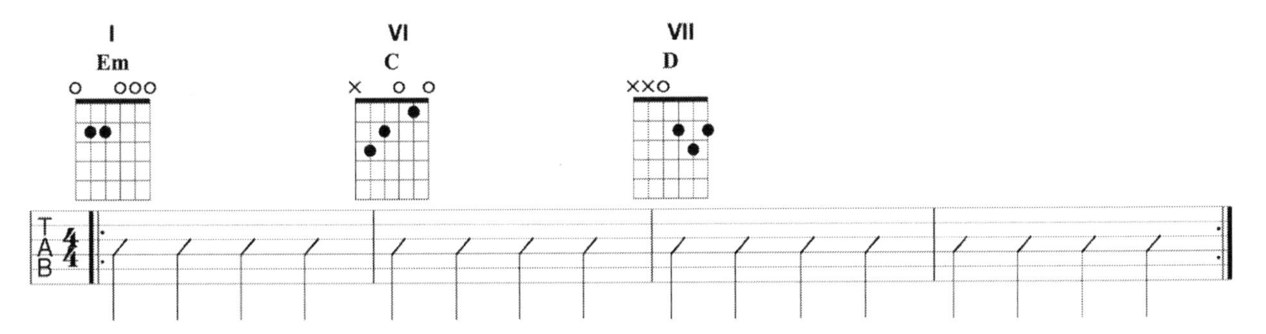

Let's add in chord **III** now. These four chords often work well together. This example is a **I-VI-III-VII** progression:

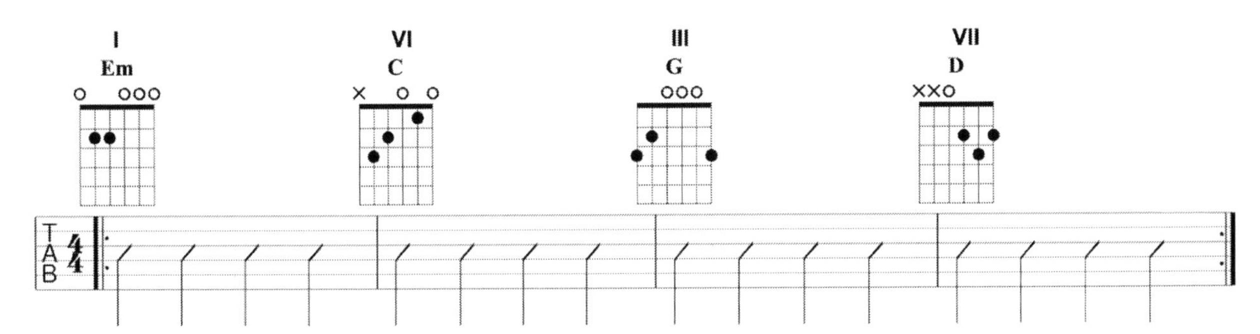

Finally let's look at some examples using chords **IV** and **V**.

This following progression uses just minor chords and is a **I-V-IV-V** sequence:

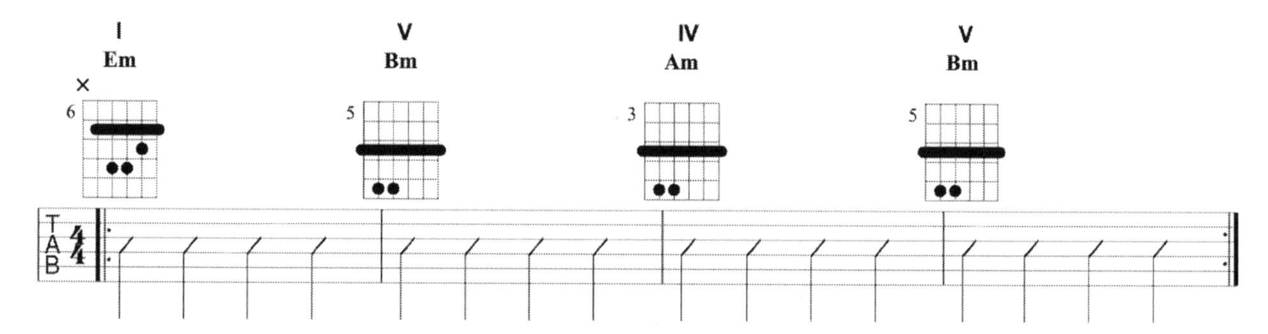

This last example uses more chords, combined into a longer sequence:

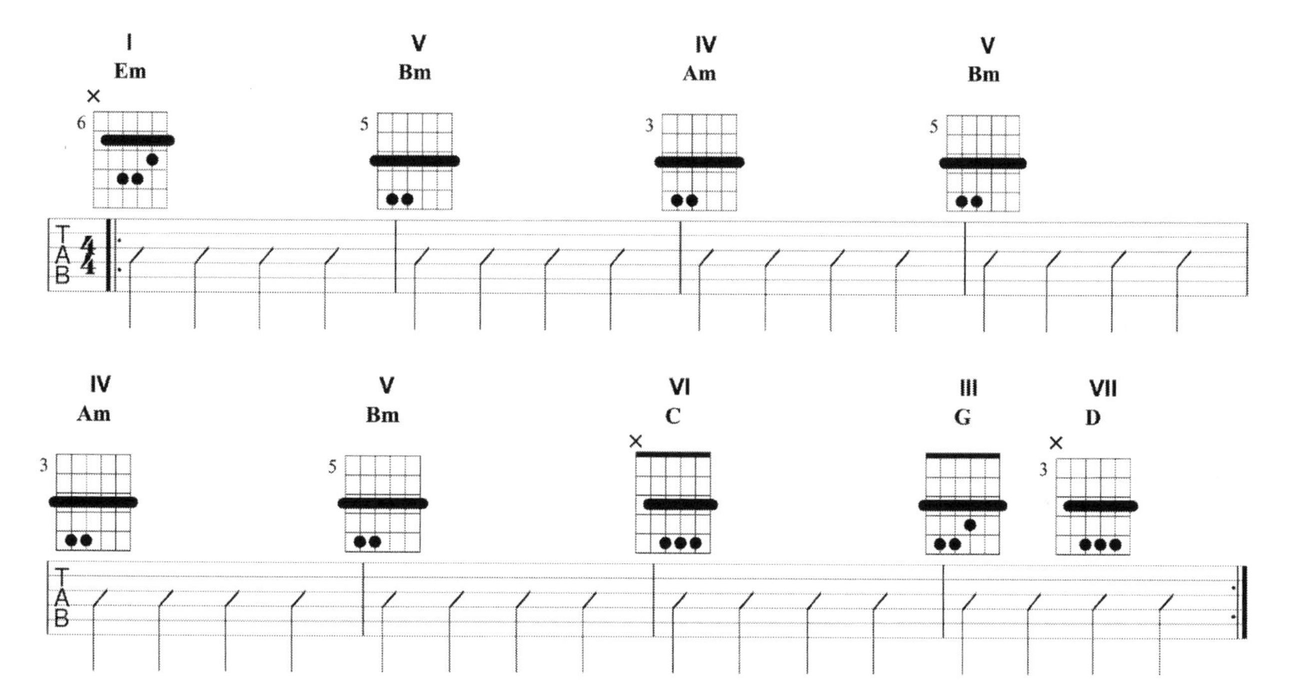

The first line of this chord progression goes **I-V-IV-V**. The second line goes **IV-V-VI-III-VII.**

Play around with these chord progressions to get an idea about how minor keys work. Then try making up some short chord progressions of your own using the chords in the key of E minor.

Breakin' the Rules...

You may have noticed some 'rules' which apply to each minor chord family:

Chords **I, IV** and **V** are ***minor***

I	II	III	IV	V	VI	VII
MINOR	DIMINISHED	MAJOR	MINOR	MINOR	MAJOR	MAJOR

Chords **III, VI** and **VII** are ***major***

I	II	III	IV	V	VI	VII
MINOR	DIMINISHED	MAJOR	MINOR	MINOR	MAJOR	MAJOR

Chord **II** is ***diminished***

I	II	III	IV	V	VI	VI
MINOR	DIMINISHED	MAJOR	MINOR	MINOR	MAJOR	MAJOR

Do these rules *always* apply?

Often, but not *always*!

Sometimes you'll see some variations on these rules.

Chord **V** is *sometimes* changed to a *major* chord. Similarly, chord **IV** is *sometimes* changed to a *major* chord.

Let's see how this might apply to the D minor chord progression we saw at the start of this chapter on minor keys. The original progression was this:

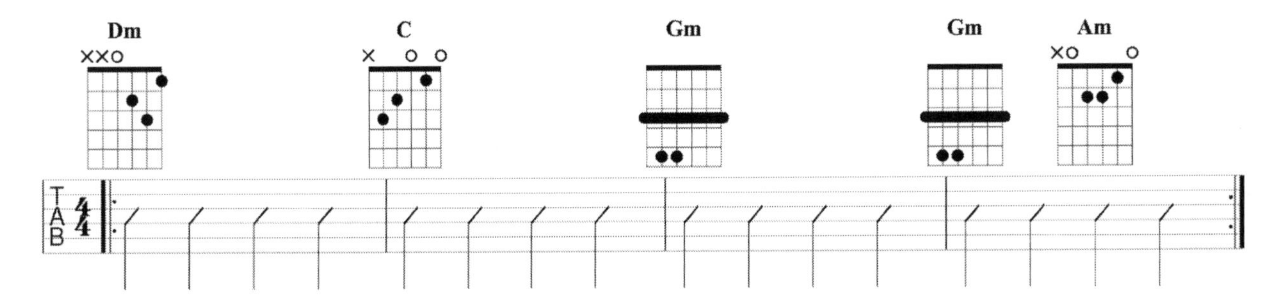

D minor is **I**, C is **VII**, Gm is **IV** and Am is **V**.

If we changed **V** to major we'd get the following:

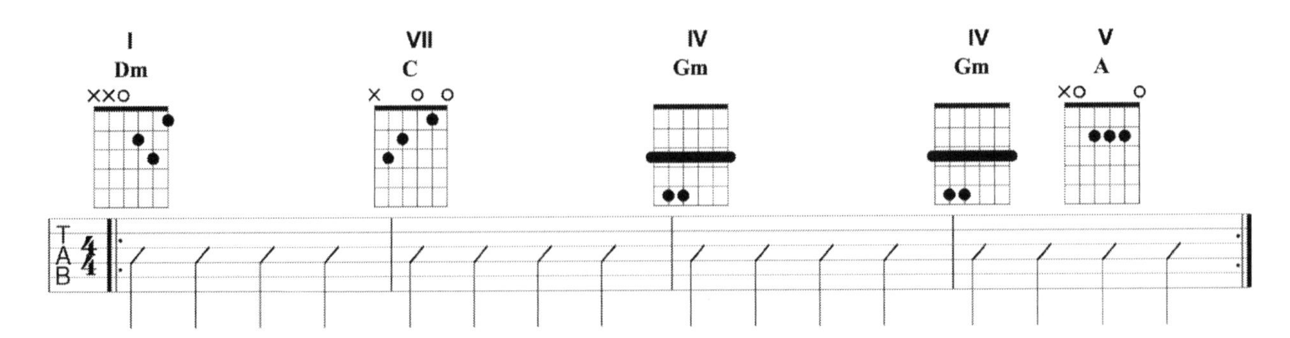

If we changed **IV** *and* **V** to major, the progression would become this:

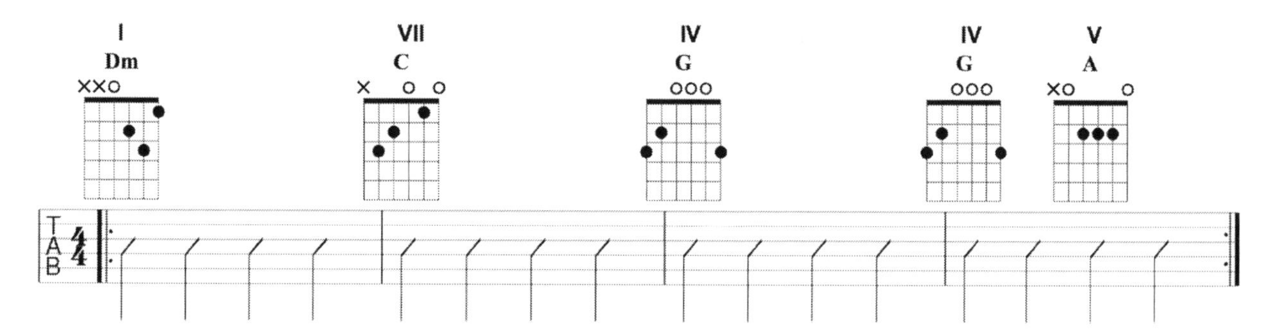

Play through these 3 examples and you'll hear that each one sounds musical, they just sound different to each other.

There are reasons why these changes work and why they're used, but we're not going to go into them now, they will be covered in more depth in books 2 & 3 in this series.

For now, just be aware of the basic chords in each minor chord family and understand that from time to time you'll see a few variations used to create a different sound.

<u>Playing Solos or Writing Melodies in Minor Keys</u>

We know that over a chord sequence in the key of G major we can write melodies, riffs or solos using the notes in the G major scale. This is because it is the 'parent scale'.

It works exactly the same in a minor key. You can use the parent **natural minor scale** over the chords in the minor chord family.

You could also use the **minor pentatonic scale**. This is because the minor pentatonic scale is just a natural minor scale with some notes removed.

These two approaches make playing in minor keys easy!

If you wanted to play a guitar solo over some chords in the key of B minor, then use the notes in the B natural minor scale or B minor pentatonic scale.

Want to write a melody over some chords in the key of G minor? Then use the notes in the G natural minor scale or G minor pentatonic scale.

If some of the chords have been changed to major like we talked about earlier, don't worry too much. This approach will still normally work. Use your ears, experiment and with practice you'll learn to navigate any little changes in the chords without any problems.

That's most of what you need to know about minor keys for now...

Now you have a solid understanding of what a minor key is, how to find the chords in a minor key, common minor key chord sequences ... and more.

There are things about minor keys which I've chosen to leave out of this chapter to stop it getting too long, complex and confusing!

What you've been shown here is the most important information, the stuff that's going to help you out 95% of the time. Once you've grasped everything in this chapter and have gained some experience using it, you will build on your minor key knowledge in books 2 & 3.

Test your understanding by answering the questions coming next. Then check your answers to see how you did.

There's a lot in this chapter so revisit bits of it as much as you need to in order for everything to make sense.

Good luck!

Now, Test Yourself on Minor Keys!

Just like major keys, each minor key has a chord family of _______ chords.

These chords come from the parent ____________________ scale.

In any major key, chord VI is the______________________. Knowing this is helpful, because the 7 chords in the chord family for any major key and its relative minor key are ______________________.

Here are the chords in the key of **D major**:

I	II	III	IV	V	VI	VII
D	Em	F#m	G	A	Bm	C#dim

Use this information to write in the chords in the **B minor** chord family:

I	II	III	IV	V	VI	VII
Bm						

Give the *chord type* or *quality* for the chords in a minor chord family:

Chords **I, IV** and **V** are ____________

Chords **III, VI** and **VII** are ____________

Chord **II** is ________________

Sometimes in minor key chord sequences the chord qualities change slightly. For example, sometimes chords **IV** or **V** are changed from _______________ to _______________ to create a different sound.

Here is a chord sequence in the key of **C# minor**:

| C#m / / / | E / / / | A / / / | B / / / |

Give the **Roman numeral** for each chord in the sequence:

C#m is _________

E is _________

A is _________

B is _________

The parent scale these chords come from is the ____________________________.

We could improvise or compose a melody over these chords using the notes in the ________________.
We could also use the __________________ pentatonic scale.

Find out how you did by checking the answers below!

Find Out How You Did!

Just like major keys, each minor key has a chord family of ***7 chords****.*

These chords come from the parent ***natural minor scale****.*

In any major key, chord VI is the ***relative minor****. Knowing this is helpful because the 7 chords in the chord family for any major key and its relative minor key are* ***the same****.*

*Here are the chords in the key of **D major**:*

I	II	III	IV	V	VI	VII
D	Em	F#m	G	A	Bm	C#dim

Chord VI, B minor is the relative minor. So, the chords in the B minor chord family will be the same, but with Bm as chord I:

I	II	III	IV	V	VI	VII
Bm	C#dim	D	Em	F#m	G	A

In any minor key chord family:

*Chords **I, IV** and **V** are **minor**.*

*Chords **III, VI** and **VII** are major.*

*Chord **II** is **diminished**.*

*Sometimes in minor key chord sequences the chord qualities change slightly. For example, sometimes chords IV or V are changed from **minor** to **major** to create a different sound.*

*Here is a chord sequence in the key of **C# minor**:*

| C#m /// | E /// | A /// | B /// |

The Roman numerals for each chord are:

***C#m** is **I**.*

***E** is **III**.*

***A** is **VI**.*

***B** is **VII**.*

*The parent scale is **C# natural minor scale.***

*We could improvise or compose a melody over these chords using the notes in the **C# natural minor scale**. We could also use the **C# minor pentatonic scale**.*

Final Words

Congratulations!

Awesome stuff...you've reached the end of the first ***Music Theory for Guitarists*** *book!*

I hope I've helped debunk some of the confusion, myths, misunderstandings and questions you had before you picked this book up.

Study each of these chapters as many times as necessary to make perfect sense of them.

Don't worry if everything doesn't instantly fall into place, with patience it will and then you'll have a much better knowledge of music theory than 99% of guitar players out there. Seems unbelievable, but it's true!

Look for all these concepts being used in the music that you play. Simple musical tools like triads, intervals and keys are behind most of the music we hear around us (yes, even *really* famous songs!).

Finally, take these concepts and experiment. Use what you have learned here. Make up chord progressions, write melodies over them, explore triads, intervals and everything else we've covered. Weave the knowledge you've gained from this book into your guitar playing and see and hear the difference it makes over time.

I hope you've enjoyed learning with me. If you'd like to continue your journey of music theory discovery, then continue on to ***Music Theory for Guitarists, Volume 2*** when you feel ready.

If you could spare five minutes to leave a review on whichever platform you bought this book from, I'd be most grateful. It helps other guitarists see if this book is right for them, and it helps me too!

Also check out the ***Useful Resources*** section at the back of this book where you can find out more about my other books, video courses and my ***Total Guitar Lab*** online membership and coaching site.

So, till next time, have fun exploring with all your new knowledge and I look forward to catching up again soon!

James

Free Video and Audio Lessons

We've created a special page on my website for readers of ***No Bull Music Theory for Guitarists***!

There you'll find links to some of my best video lessons to help you explore and apply some of the ideas presented in this book.

Discover more on topics like playing scales, rock and blues pentatonic licks, natural minor licks, power chords, the major pentatonic scale and more!

You'll also find the free audio lessons that accompany this book there.

Learn more at: **jamesshipwayguitar.com/theory**

Useful Chord Shapes

Here you'll find some useful open chord and barre chord shapes.

You can use these, or other shapes you already know to play some of the examples in ***No Bull Music Theory*** on your guitar.

<u>**Open Chords**</u>

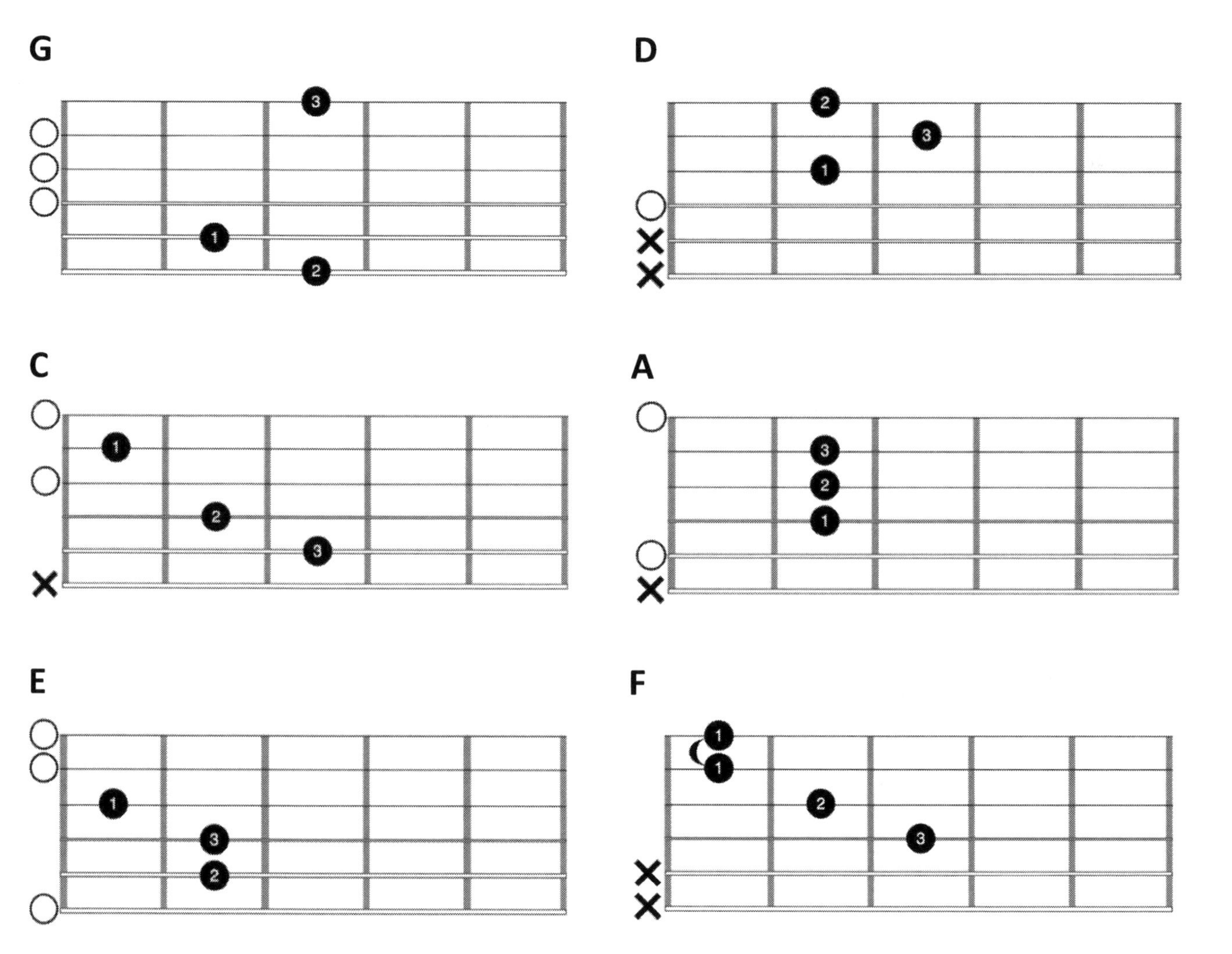

Em

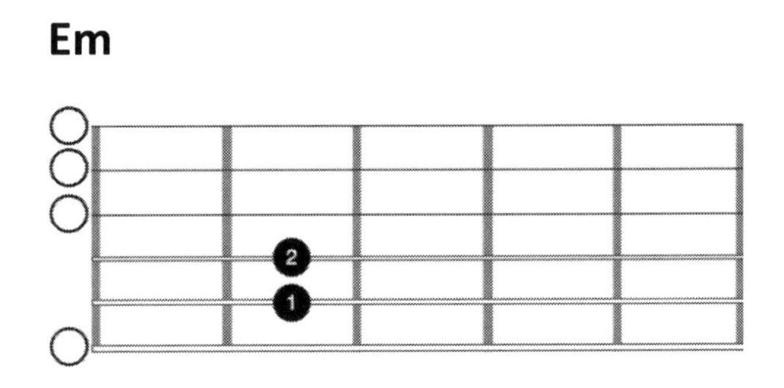

Am

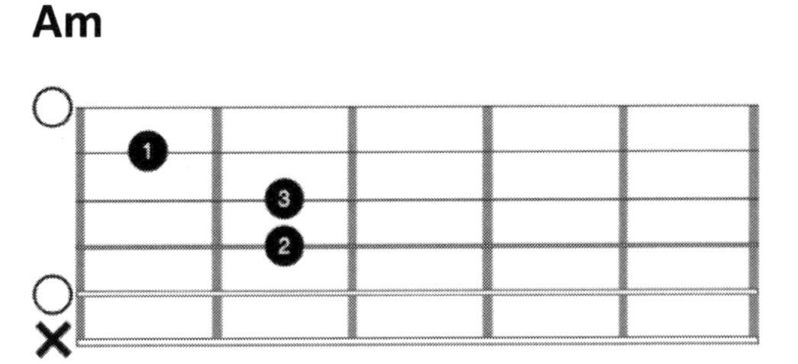

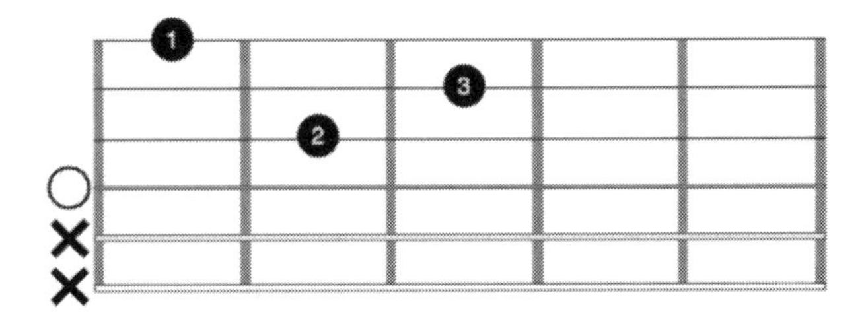

Barre Chords

Using these barre chord shapes you can play *any* major or minor chord you want. That's why barre chords are such a useful tool for guitarists!

If you haven't used barre chords before then they take practice and strength to master. Persevere and you'll find it's worth the effort.

Barre Chords with Root on E String

Use this shape for a **major** chord:

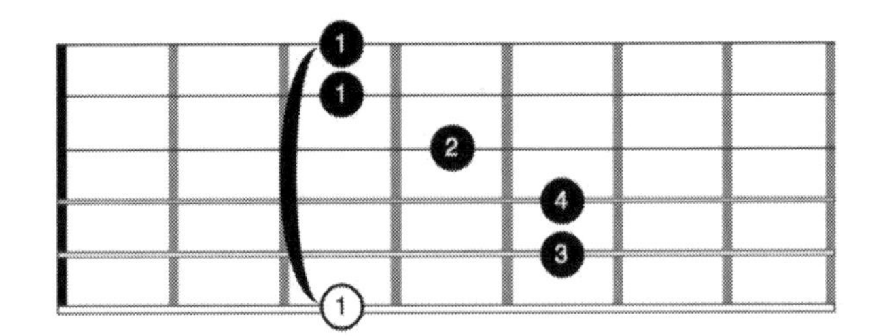

Use this shape for a **minor** chord:

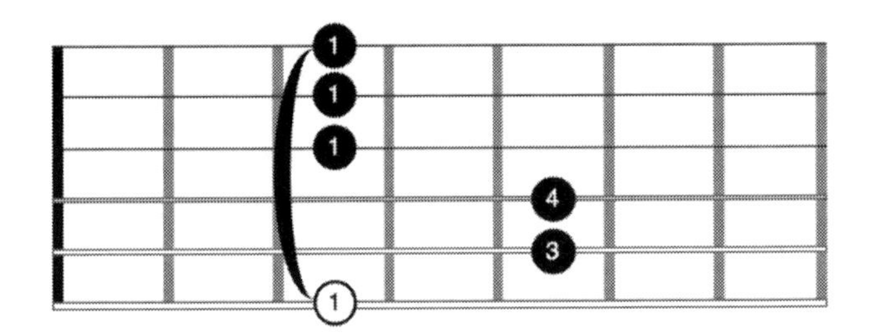

Here are the notes along the **E string**:

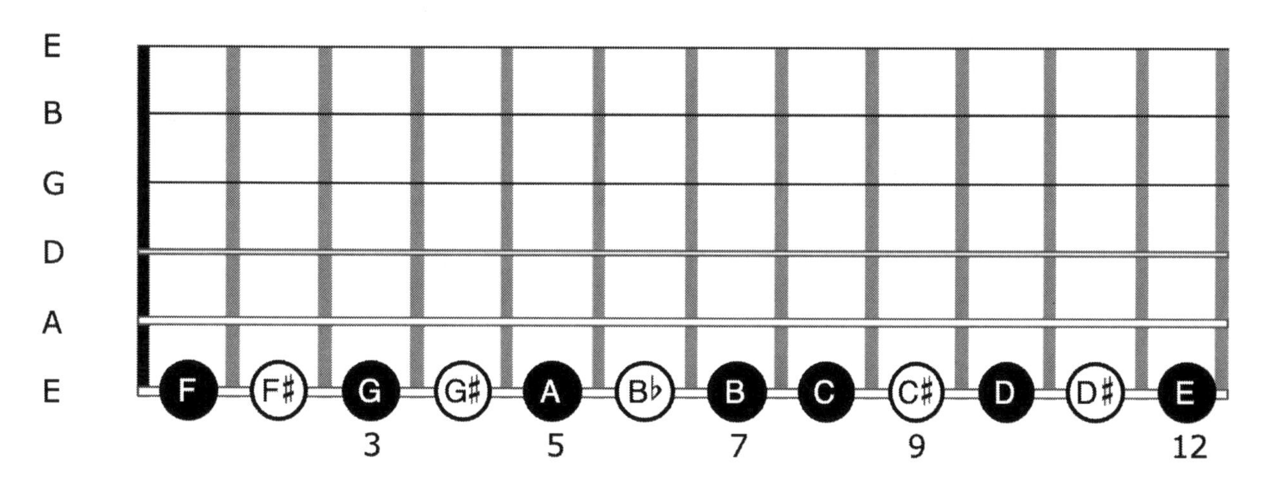

Here's how to use these shapes:

Look at the notes on the **E** string. Find the note you need for the chord you want to play
Now move the chord shape along the neck so that the barre is placed across this fret. Remember to use the major shape if you want a major chord and the minor shape if you want a minor chord!

For example:

To play a **B major** chord find the note **B** on the E string (7th fret). Move the **major** barre chord shape along to the 7th fret and you get a B chord:

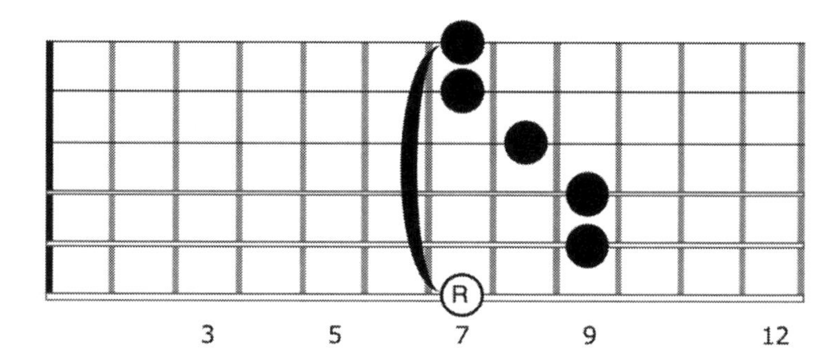

To play a **G minor** chord find **G** on the E string (3rd fret). Move the **minor** barre chord shape along to the 3rd fret and you get a Gm chord:

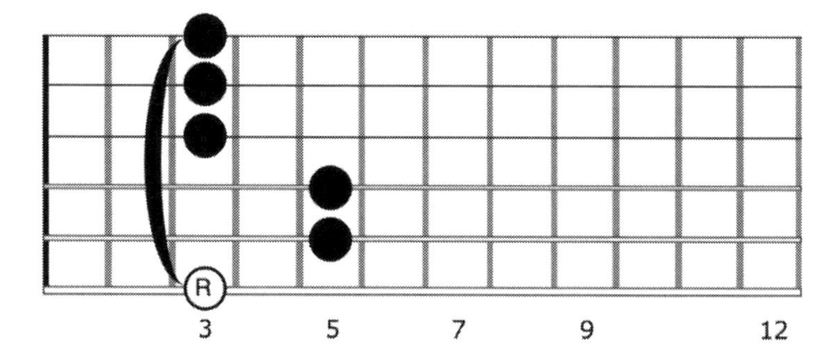

Barre Chords with Root on A String

Use for a **major** chord:

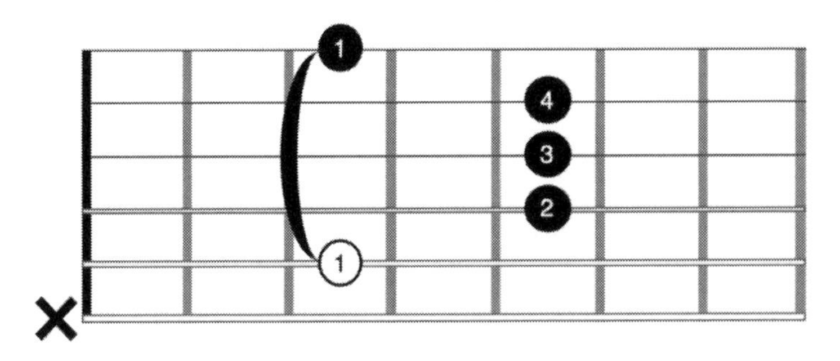

If you find this fingering awkward you might prefer barring the D, G and B strings with your 3rd finger like this:

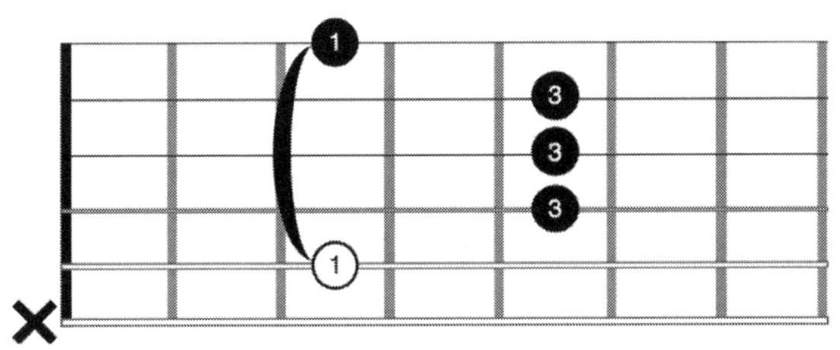

Both these fingerings may take a little practice, the secret is just to persevere!

Use this shape for a **minor** chord:

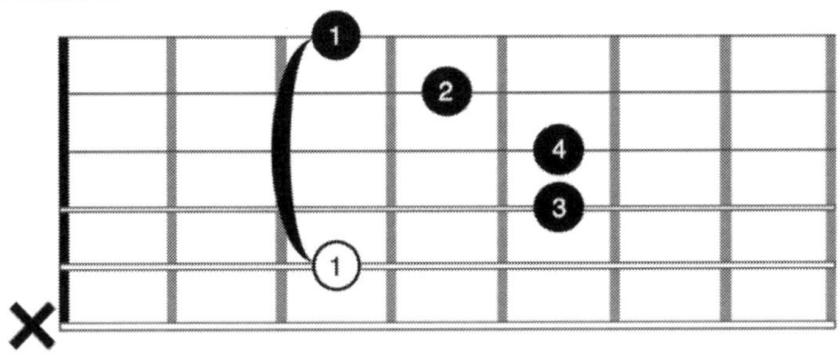

Here are the notes along the **A string**:

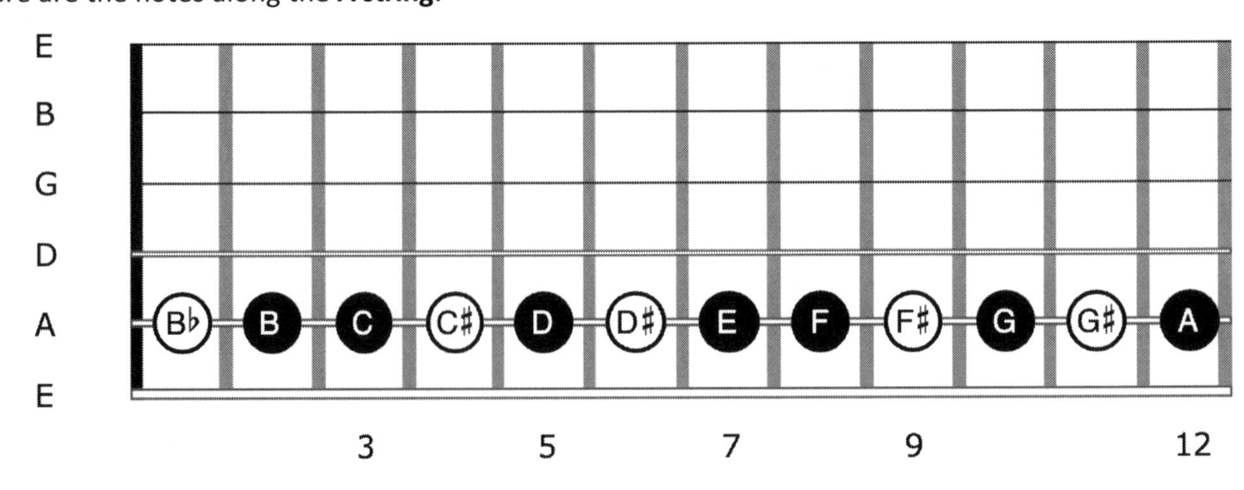

To use these shapes:

Look at the notes on the **A** string.

Find the note you need for the chord you want to play.

Now move the chord shape along the neck so that the barre is placed along this fret.

Remember to use the major shape if you want a major chord and the minor shape if you want a minor chord!

For example:

To play a **D major** chord find the note **D** on the A string (5th fret). Move the **major** barre chord shape along to the 5th fret and you get a D chord:

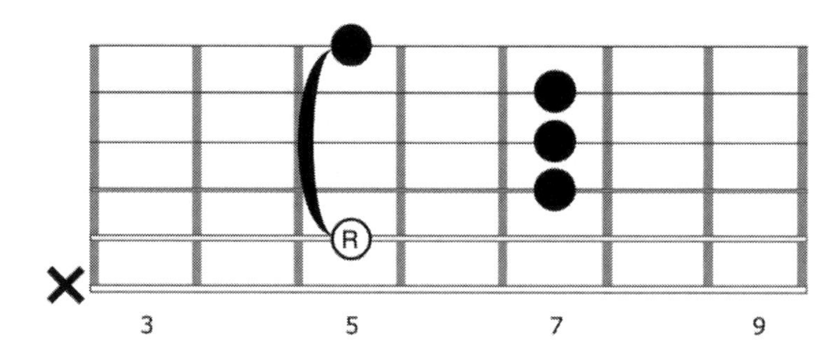

To play a **C# minor** chord find **C#** on the A string (4th fret). Move the **minor** barre chord shape along to the 4th fret and you get a C#m chord:

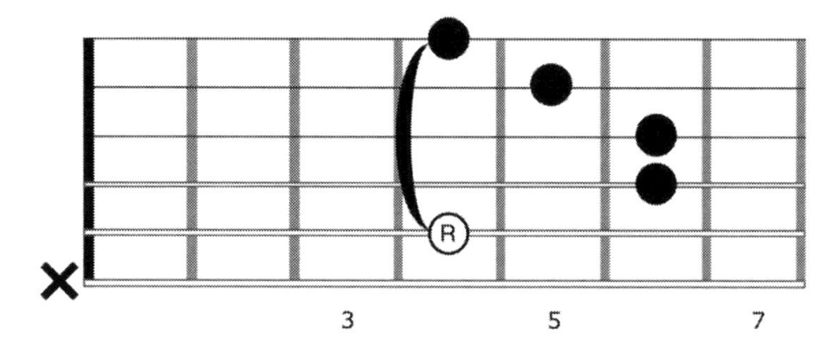

Useful Resources

Other Books by James Shipway:

Below you will find a list of my other guitar books. To find out more about each one, or to see where you can order from, please visit Headstock Books at:

headstockbooks.com

Most titles are available as paperbacks, ebooks and hardcovers from Amazon, Apple, Google Play, Kobo, Barnes & Noble, and by request from your local library or book shop.

'Music Theory for Guitarists, Volume 2'

Continue your journey towards music theory and guitar fretboard mastery with the second book in the ***Music Theory for Guitarists*** series. Discover 'sus' and 'add9' chords, compound intervals, seventh chords, key signatures, the modes of the major scale, triad chord inversions, using the circle of fifths and much more. Packed full of practical exercises and examples and **includes downloadable play-along tracks**.

'Music Theory for Guitarists, Volume 3'

Take your music theory expertise and understanding of the guitar fretboard *even* further with the third book in the ***Music Theory for Guitarists*** series! Learn about the CAGED System, soloing with modes, chord substitution tricks and techniques, minor key progressions and improvisation, the harmonic minor scale, extended chords, key change and modulation techniques and much more. Packed full of practical exercises and examples and **includes downloadable play-along tracks**.

'No Bull Barre Chords for Guitar'

Discover a step-by-step system for mastering the **essential barre chord shapes** that *all* guitarists and singer-songwriter guitar players need to know! You'll learn the most important and useful barre chord shapes and how to use them to play literally *hundreds* of possible chord sequences and songs. *Plus,* you'll discover powerful practice methods, exercises and 'memory hacks' to help you master barre chords without the headaches most players face. **Free downloadable play-along practice tracks** included.

'Blues Soloing for Guitar', Volumes 1 & 2

Volume 1: 'Blues Basics' A step-by-step introduction for learning to play blues guitar, featuring the essential techniques, scales and theory you need to know, as well as complete solos in the styles of important blues legends.

Volume 2: 'Levelling Up' This book carries on where Volume 1 leaves off. It features lessons on minor blues soloing, open string soloing and scales, Texas blues style and 'jazzy' blues sounds and more.

Both books include access to a supporting website with **video lessons and audio downloads**.

'The CAGED System for Guitar'

A step-by-step method showing you how to master the guitar fretboard using the CAGED System to become a better lead player, improviser and all round guitarist.

Discover how the CAGED System works and how to use it to learn all the scales and arpeggios you need to know to become an awesome guitar player. With crystal clear explanations, practice exercises and tips, 'speed learning' techniques, as well as dozens of exciting sample licks, '**The CAGED System for Guitar**' can seriously transform your playing skills. Includes **downloadable video demonstrations and backing tracks**.

'Circle of Fifths for Guitar'

Discover the awesome power of the circle of fifths and use it to **boost your guitar skills, music theory knowledge, song writing skills** ...and more! Bite-sized lessons showing you how to use the circle of fifths to memorise the notes on the guitar fretboard, practice smarter for faster progress, learn the chords in every major and minor key, change keys quickly and easily, understand chord progressions and songs, and much more. With practical exercises and quizzes to check your understanding. Includes a downloadable **circle of fifths video masterclass**!

'The Guitar Practice Workbook'

The ultimate '**multi-purpose**' **practice workbook** for guitarists of all levels. Featuring powerful practice hacks, important scales and chord shapes as well as over 50 pages of blank tab, fretboard diagrams and chord boxes for recording your own killer licks, exercises and song ideas! Available with **free downloadable 'Goal Worksheet'** to help you track your progress and reach your guitar goals! Available as a paperback only.

Check Out My *Total Guitar Lab* Online School

Want to study specific guitar styles and topics with me as your guitar teacher? Well you can, with my online guitar community **Total Guitar Lab**! Join and get instant access to *all* my premium guitar courses *plus* live training, workshops and Q&A sessions. Learn more and discover the amazing results guitarists have been getting with my training. Visit **totalguitarlab.com**

Single Courses Also Available:

Some of my guitar courses are available as stand-alone products. This means they are yours to keep and go through at your own pace as many times as you like.

Courses are made up of step-by-step video lessons, downloadable backing tracks, audio lessons and detailed tab workbooks complete with homework tasks and checklists to make sure you reach your goals.

The following courses are currently available. You can find them at **totalguitarlab.com** :

Blues Guitar Launchpad

The perfect course for the beginner to intermediate electric blues guitarist. Learn all the essential blues scales, how to play the 12 bar blues, authentic blues licks, string bending and vibrato techniques plus complete solo studies in the styles of blues legends like Eric Clapton, Stevie Ray Vaughan, Freddie King, Otis Rush and others! Learn more at: **totalguitarlab.com**

Minor Pentatonic Mastery

Perfect for the more experienced rock or blues player who wants to conquer the minor pentatonic scale all over the guitar neck! ***Minor Pentatonic Mastery*** takes you step-by-step through all the ways to play the minor pentatonic scale on the guitar. Learn all 5 'box patterns' and how to use them to play killer blues and rock licks, discover 'sliding' scale patterns, the 'Rule of 2' to use for connecting it all up and loads more powerful soloing and improvising tips to use in building an awesome pentatonic soloing vocabulary. Learn more at: **totalguitarlab.com**

Rock Guitar Lick Lab

Aimed at the intermediate rock guitar player who wants to explode their playing with the licks and techniques used by the biggest names in rock and metal guitar. Discover essential rock bending licks, repeating licks, alternate picked licks, extended blues scale licks and stretch and sequence licks and how to use them in your playing for explosive rock and metal guitar solos!

You'll also learn essential technique tips to get the licks sounding great and how to use everything in the course to easily start generating killer rock licks of your own. Learn more at: **totalguitarlab.com**

Solo Blues Jamming Workshop

Learn a step-by-step method for combining chords and licks into your very own solo blues jams! Includes play-a-long tracks, drill videos and more to help you master this fun way of playing blues guitar. Learn more at: **totalguitarlab.com**

Notebuster

Want to learn all the notes on the fretboard in the quickest and most pain free way possible? ***Notebuster*** will show you how! After this short mini course, you'll be able to find *any* note on *any* string ... *anywhere* on the guitar. Learn more at: **totalguitarlab.com**

Follow me on YouTube:

Search for James Shipway Guitar on YouTube and subscribe for hours of free video lessons!

No Bull Music Theory for Guitarists
by James Shipway

Published by Headstock Books
headstockbooks.com

Paperback ISBN: 978-1-914453-10-6
Hardcover ISBN: 978-1-914453-12-0 / 978-1-914453-13-7
Ebook ISBN: 978-1-914453-11-3

Made in the USA
Las Vegas, NV
14 January 2025